Wine Basics FOR DUMMIES®

by Ed McCarthy and
Mary Ewing-Mulligan MW

Wiley Publishing, Inc.

Wine Basics For Dummies®

Published by
Wiley Publishing, Inc.
111 River St.
Hoboken, NJ 07030-5774
www.wiley.com

Published by Wiley Publishing, Inc., Indianapolis, Indiana

For general information on our other products and services, please contact our Customer Care Department within the U.S. at 800-762-2974, outside the U.S. at 317-572-3993, or fax 317-572-4002.

For technical support, please visit www.wiley.com/techsupport.

ISBN-13: 978-0-7645-7991-2

ISBN-10: 0-7645-7991-6

Manufactured in the United States of America

1O/SR/QT/QV/IN

Publisher's Acknowledgments

Senior Project Editor: Zoë Wykes
Technical Editor: Christopher Cree MW
Editorial Manager: Rev Mengle
Brand Development Representative: Stephanie Corby
Cartoon: Rich Tennant, www.the5thwave.com
Special Art: © 2003 Akira Chiwaki

For information about a custom Dummies book for your company or organization, contact BrandedRights&Licenses@wiley.com.

About the Authors

Ed McCarthy and **Mary Ewing-Mulligan** are two wine lovers who met at an Italian wine tasting in New York City's Chinatown in 1981. Two years later, they formally merged their wine cellars and wine libraries when they married. They have since coauthored six wine books in the *Wine For Dummies* series of books (including their latest two, *French Wine For Dummies* and *Italian Wine For Dummies*), taught hundreds of wine classes together, visited nearly every wine region in the world, run five marathons, and raised ten cats. Along the way, they have amassed more than half a century of professional wine experience between them.

Table of Contents

"Oh, come on, you're just drinking it! You're not even tasting it..."

Chapter 1

Wine 101

In This Chapter

- What wine is
- Fifty-cent words like *fermentation* and *tannin*
- What red wine has that white wine doesn't
- The blushing truth about rosés
- Differences between table wine, sparkling wine, and fortified wine

Welcome to *Wine Basics For Dummies.* Before we get started with the meat (okay, the grape) of this book, you need to know something about us. We love wine. We love the way it tastes, we love the fascinating variety of wines in the world, and we love the way wine brings people together at the dinner table. We believe that you too should be able to enjoy wine — regardless of your experience or your budget.

But we'll be the first to admit that wine people, such as many wine professionals and really serious connoisseurs, don't make it easy for regular people to enjoy wine. You have to know strange names of grape varieties. You have to figure out whether to buy a $16 wine or a $6 wine. You even need a special tool to open the bottle after you get it home!

All this complication surrounding wine will never go away, because wine is a very rich and complex field. But you don't have to let that stand in your way. With a little understanding of what wine is, you can begin to buy and enjoy wine.

First, about This Book

One of the best things about this book, or any *For Dummies* book for that matter, is the fact that this book is a textbook of sorts, a user's manual, and a reference book, all in one. In *Wine Basics For Dummies,* we include basic information about wine for readers who know nothing (or next to nothing) about wine — and we give you tips and suggestions that will have you feeling like a seasoned wine drinker in no time. Depending on where you fall on the wine-knowledge gradient, different chapters will be relevant to you.

Feel free to start wherever you want and move around at your leisure. Here's a little guidance to get you started:

- If having the correct vocabulary to talk and taste wine intriques you, then seek and ye shall find in Chapter 2.
- If you've wrangled a time or two with a corkscrew (and always lost the fight), you're sure to turn victor by thumbing through some of Chapter 6.
- And, if you've always wanted to know what wines taste best with which foods, go immediately to Chapter 7. Yes, we said immediately.

Wherever you jump in, you're sure to see little icons here and there. Here's what the icons mean:

Where you see this little guy, feel free to skip over the technical information that follows. Wine will still taste just as delicious.

Advice and information that will make you a wiser wine drinker or buyer is marked by this bull's-eye so that you won't miss it.

There's very little you can do in the course of moderate wine consumption that can land you in jail — but you could spoil an expensive bottle and sink into a deep depression over your loss. This symbol warns you about common pitfalls.

Some issues in wine are so fundamental that they bear repeating. Just so you don't think we repeated ourselves without realizing it, we mark the repetitions with this symbol.

Wine snobs practice all sorts of affectations designed to make other wine drinkers feel inferior. But you won't be intimidated by their snobbery if you see it for what it is.

Unfortunately, some of the finest, most intriguing, most delicious wines are made in very small quantities. Usually, those wines cost more than wines made in large quantities — but that's not the only problem; the real frustration is that those wines have very limited distribution, and you can't always get your hands on a bottle even if you're willing to pay the price. We mark such wines with this icon and hope that your search proves fruitful.

Wine Is for Everyone

Because we hate to think that wine, which has brought so much pleasure into our lives, could be the source of anxiety for anyone, we want to help you feel more comfortable around wine. Some knowledge of wine, gleaned from the pages of this book and from our shared experiences, will go a long way toward increasing your comfort level.

But ironically, what will *really* make you feel comfortable about wine is accepting the fact that you'll never know it all — and that you've got *plenty* of company.

You see, after you really get a handle on wine, you discover that *no one* knows everything there is to know about wine. And when you know that, you can just relax and enjoy the stuff.

How Wine Happens

We've found that two types of wine lovers appear to exist in the world: the *hedonists,* who just want to enjoy wine and find more and more wines they can enjoy; and the *thinkers,* who are fascinated by how wine happens. Our family has one of each.

If you're a thinker, you'll enjoy discovering what's behind the differences in wines. And even if you're a hedonist, a little knowledge can help you discover more wines that you'll enjoy. Of course, this is the thinker speaking.

The recipe for turning fruit into wine goes sort of like this:

1. **Pick a large quantity of ripe grapes from grapevines.** You could substitute raspberries or any other fruit, but 99.9 percent of all the wine in the world is made from grapes, because they make the best wines.
2. **Put the grapes into a clean container that doesn't leak.**
3. **Crush the grapes somehow to release their juice.** Once upon a time, feet performed this function.
4. **Wait.**

In its most basic form, winemaking is that simple. After the grapes are crushed, *yeasts* (tiny one-celled organisms that exist naturally in the vineyard and, therefore, on the grapes) come into contact with the sugar in the grapes' juice and gradually convert that sugar into alcohol. Yeasts also produce carbon dioxide, which evaporates into the air. When the yeasts are done working, your grape juice is wine. The sugar that was in the juice is no longer there — alcohol is present instead. (The riper and sweeter the grapes, the more alcohol the wine will have.) This process is called *fermentation.*

What could be more natural? Fermentation is a totally natural process that doesn't require man's participation at all, except to put the grapes into a container and release the juice from the grapes. For example, fermentation occurs in fresh apple cider left too long in your refrigerator, without any help from you.

Modern wrinkles in winemaking

Today's winemakers can control the type of container they use for the fermentation process (stainless steel and oak are the two main materials), as well as the size of the container and the temperature of the juice during fermentation — and every one of these choices can make a big difference in the taste of the wine. After fermentation, winemakers can choose how long to let the wine *mature* (a stage when the wine sort of gets its act together) and in what kind of container. Fermentation can last three days or three months, and the wine can then mature for a couple of months or a couple of years or anything in between. If you have trouble making decisions, don't ever become a winemaker.

The main ingredient

Obviously, one of the biggest factors in making one wine different from the next is the nature of the raw material, the grape juice. Besides the fact that riper, sweeter grapes make a more alcoholic wine, different *varieties* of grapes (Chardonnay, Cabernet Sauvignon, or Merlot, for example) make different wines. Grapes are the main ingredient in wine, and everything the winemaker does, he does to the particular grape juice he has. Chapter 3 covers specific grapes and the kinds of wine they make.

What Color Is Your Appetite?

Your inner child will be happy to know that when it comes to wine, it's okay to like some colors more than others. You can't get away with saying "I don't like green food!" beyond your sixth birthday, but you can express a general preference for white, red, or pink wine for all your adult years.

(Not exactly) white wine

Whoever coined the term "white wine" must have been colorblind. All you have to do is look at it to see that it's not white, it's yellow. But we've all gotten used to the expression by now, and so *white wine* it is. (Let's hope that person didn't live in a snowy city.)

White wine is wine without any red color (or pink color, which is in the red family). This means that *White Zinfandel,* a popular pink wine, isn't white wine. But yellow wines, golden wines, and wines that are as pale as water are all white wines.

Wondering what happens to the grape skins during the winemaking process? The skins are removed from the grapes by either *pressing* large quantities of grapes so that the juice flows out and the skins stay behind — like squeezing the pulp out of grapes the way kids do in the cafeteria — or by *crushing* the grapes in a machine with a huge screw that breaks the skins and lets the juice drain away.

Is white always right?

You can drink white wine anytime you like — which for most people means as a drink without food or with lighter foods.

White wines are often considered *apéritif* wines, meaning wines consumed before dinner, in place of cocktails, or at parties. (If you ask the officials who busy themselves defining such things, an apéritif wine is a wine that has flavors added to it. But unless you're in the business of writing wine labels for a living, don't worry about that. In common parlance, an apéritif wine is just what we said.)

Lots of people like to drink white wines when the weather is hot because they're more refreshing than red wines, and they are usually drunk chilled (the wines, not the people).

White wines are served cool, but not ice-cold. Sometimes restaurants serve white wines too cold, and you actually have to wait a while for the wine to warm up before you drink it. If you like your wine cold, fine; but try drinking your favorite white wine a little less cold sometime, and you'll discover the wine has more flavor that way.

For suggestions of foods to eat with white wine, turn to Chapter 7; for really detailed information about white wine and food (and white wine itself, for that matter), refer to our book *White Wine For Dummies* (Wiley).

Popular white wines

These types of white wine are available almost everywhere in the U.S.

- **Chardonnay:** Can come from California, Australia, France, or almost any other place
- **Sauvignon Blanc:** Can come from California, France, New Zealand, South Africa, and other places
- **Riesling:** Can come from Germany, California, New York, Washington, France, Austria, Australia, and other places
- **Pinot Grigio** or **Pinot Gris:** Can come from Italy, France, Oregon, California, and other places
- **Soave:** Comes from Italy

Red, red wine

In this case, the name is correct. Red wines really are red. They can be purple red, ruby red, or garnet, but they're red.

The most obvious difference between red wine and white wine is color. The red color occurs when the colorless juice of red grapes stays in contact with the dark grape skins during fermentation and absorbs the skins' color. Along with color, the grape skins give the wine *tannin,* a substance that's an important part of the way a red wine tastes. (See Chapter 2 for more about the taste of tannin.) The presence of tannin in red wines is actually the most important taste difference between red wines and white wines.

Red wines vary in style more than white wines do. This is partly because winemakers have more ways of adjusting their red-winemaking to achieve the kind of wine they want. For example, if winemakers leave the juice in contact with the skins for a long time, the wine becomes more *tannic* (firmer in the mouth, like strong tea; tannic wines can make you pucker). If winemakers drain the juice off the skins sooner, the wine is softer and less tannic.

Red wine tends to be consumed more often as part of a meal than as a drink on its own.

Thanks to the wide range of red wine styles, you can find red wines to go with just about every type of food and every occasion when you want to drink wine (except the times when you want to drink a wine with bubbles, because most bubbly wines are white or pink). In Chapter 7, we give you some tips on matching red wine with food. You can also consult our book about red wine, *Red Wine For Dummies* (Wiley).

One sure way to spoil the fun in drinking most red wines is to drink them cold. Those tannins can taste really bitter when the wine is cold — just as in a cold glass of very strong tea. On the other hand, many restaurants serve red wines too warm. If the bottle feels cool to your hand, that's a good temperature. For more about serving wine at the right temperature, see Chapter 6.

Popular red wines

You'll find descriptions and explanations of these popular and widely available red wines all through this book.

- **Cabernet Sauvignon:** Can come from California, Australia, France, and other places
- **Merlot:** Can come from California, France, Washington, New York, Chile, and other places
- **Pinot Noir:** Can come from California, France, Oregon, New Zealand, and other places
- **Beaujolais:** Comes from France
- **Lambrusco:** Usually comes from Italy
- **Chianti:** Comes from Italy
- **Zinfandel:** Usually comes from California
- **Côtes du Rhône:** Comes from France
- **Bordeaux:** Comes from France

A rose is a rose, but a rosé is "white"

Rosé wines are pink wines. Rosé wines are made from red grapes, but they don't end up red because the grape juice stays in contact with the red skins for a very short time — only a few hours, compared to days or weeks for red wines. Because this *skin contact* (the period when the juice and the skins intermingle) is brief, rosé wines absorb very little tannin from the skins. Therefore, you can chill rosé wines and drink them as you would white wines.

Of course, not all rosé wines are called rosés. (That would be too simple.) Many rosé wines today are called *blush* wines — a term invented by wine marketers to avoid the word *rosé,* because back in the '80s pink wines weren't very popular. Lest someone figures out that *blush* is a synonym for *rosé,* the labels call these wines *white.* But even a child can see that White Zinfandel is really pink.

The blush wines that call themselves *white* are fairly sweet. Wines labeled *rosé* can be sweetish, too, but some wonderful rosés from Europe (and a few from America) are *dry* (not sweet). Although hard-core wine lovers hardly ever drink rosé wine, we love to drink dry rosés in the summer.

Other Ways of Categorizing Wine

We have a game we sometimes play with our friends. "Which wine," we ask them, "would you want to have with you if you were stranded on a desert island?" In other words, which wine could you drink for the rest of your life without getting tired of it? Our own answer is always Champagne, with a capital *C* (more on the capitalization later in this section).

In a way, Champagne is an odd choice because, as much as we love it, we don't drink Champagne *every day* under normal circumstances. What we do drink daily is regular wine — red, white, or pink — without bubbles. These wines come with various names; in America, they're called *table* wines, and in Europe they're called *light* wines. Sometimes these wines are referred to as *still* wines, because they don't have bubbles moving around inside them.

In the following sections, we explain the differences within these three categories of wines: table wines, dessert wines, and sparkling wines.

Table wine

Table wine, or *light wine,* is fermented grape juice whose alcohol content falls within a certain range. Furthermore, table wine is not bubbly. (Some table wines have a very slight carbonation, but not enough to disqualify them as table wines.) According to U.S. standards of identification, table wines may have an alcohol content no higher than 14 percent; in Europe, light wine must contain from 8.5 percent to 14 percent alcohol by volume (with a few exceptions). So unless a wine has more than 14 percent alcohol or has bubbles, the wine is a *table wine* or a *light wine* in the eyes of the law.

The regulations-makers didn't get the number 14 by drawing it from a hat. Historically, most wines contained less than

14 percent alcohol — either because there wasn't enough sugar in the juice to attain a higher alcohol level, or because the yeasts died off when the alcohol reached 14 percent, halting the fermentation. That number, therefore, became the legal borderline between wines that have no alcohol added to them (table wines) and wines that do have alcohol added (see "Dessert wine," in the next section).

Here's our own, real-world definition of table wines: They are the normal, non-bubbly wines that *most* people drink *most* of the time.

Dessert wine

Many wines have more than 14 percent alcohol because alcohol was added during or after the fermentation. That's an unusual way of making wine, but some parts of the world, like the Sherry region in Spain and the Port region in Portugal, have made quite a specialty of it.

Dessert wine is the legal U.S. terminology for these wines, probably because they're usually sweet and often enjoyed after dinner. We find that term misleading, because dessert wines are not *always* sweet and not *always* consumed after dinner. (Dry Sherry is categorized as a dessert wine, for example, but it's dry, and we drink it before dinner.)

In Europe, this category of wines is called *liqueur wines,* which carries the same connotation of sweetness. We prefer the term *fortified,* which suggests that the wine has been strengthened with additional alcohol. But until we get elected to run things, the term will have to be *dessert wine* or *liqueur wine.*

Sparkling wine (and a highly personal spelling lesson)

Sparkling wines are wines that contain carbon dioxide bubbles. Carbon dioxide gas is a natural byproduct of fermentation, and winemakers sometimes decide to trap the gas in the wine. Just about every country that makes wine also makes sparkling wine.

How to (sort of) learn the alcohol content of a wine

Regulations require wineries to state a wine's alcohol percentage on the label (again, with some minor exceptions). It can be expressed in *degrees,* like 12.5 degrees, or as a percentage, like 12.5 percent. If a wine carries the words "Table Wine" on its label in the U.S., but not the alcohol percentage, it should have less than 14 percent alcohol by law.

For wines sold within the U.S. — whether the wine is American or imported — there's a big catch, however. The labels are allowed to lie. U.S. regulations give wineries a 1.5 percent leeway in the accuracy of the alcohol level. If the label states 12.5 percent, the actual alcohol level can be as high as 14 percent or as low as 11 percent. The leeway does not entitle the wineries to exceed the 14 percent maximum, however.

If the alcohol percentage is stated as a number that's neither a full number nor a half-number — 12.8 or 13.2, for example, instead of 12.5 or 13 — odds are it's precise.

In the U.S., Canada, and Europe, *sparkling wine* is the official name for the category of wines with bubbles. Isn't it nice when everyone agrees?

Champagne (with a capital C) is the most famous sparkling wine — and probably the most famous *wine,* for that matter. Champagne is a specific type of sparkling wine (made from certain grape varieties and produced in a certain way) that comes from a region in France called Champagne. Champagne is the undisputed Grand Champion of Bubblies.

Unfortunately for the people of Champagne, France, their wine is so famous that the name *champagne* has been borrowed again and again by producers elsewhere, until the word has become synonymous with practically the whole category of sparkling wines. In the U.S., for example, winemakers can legally call any sparkling wine *champagne* — even with a capital C, if they want — as long as the carbonation was not added artificially. (They do have to add a qualifying geographic term such as *American* or *Californian* before the word Champagne, however.)

For the French, limiting the use of the name *champagne* to the wines of the Champagne region has become a *cause célèbre.* European Union regulations not only prevent any other member country from calling its sparkling wines *champagne* but also prohibit the use of terms that even *suggest* the word *champagne,* such as fine print on the label saying that a wine was made using the "champagne method." What's more, bottles of sparkling wine from countries outside the European Union that use the word *champagne* on the label are banned from sale in Europe. The French are that serious.

To us, this seems perfectly fair. You'll never catch us using the word *champagne* as a generic term for wine with bubbles. We have too much respect for the people and the traditions of Champagne, France, where the best sparkling wines in the world are made. That's why we stress the capital C when we say Champagne. *Those* are the wines we want on our desert island, not just any sparkling wine that calls itself champagne and comes from any old place.

When someone tries to impress you by serving a "Champagne" that's not French, don't be impressed. In places such as the U.S. where calling sparkling wines champagne is legal, usually only inexpensive, low-quality wines actually use that name. Most of the top sparkling wine companies in America, for example, won't call their wines champagne — even though legally they can — out of respect for their French counterparts.

Chapter 2

These Taste Buds Are for You

In This Chapter

- How to slurp and gurgle
- Aromas you can smell in wine
- The taste of acidity, tannin, and wild strawberries
- Wine can have backbone and body
- Six mysterious concepts of wine quality

Our friends who are normal people (as opposed to our friends who are wine people) like to mock us when we do things like bring our own wine to a party or drive all the way from New York to Boston to go wine shopping. Most of the time, we don't even try to defend ourselves. We realize how ridiculous our behavior must seem.

In our early days as wine drinkers, we, too, used to think that all wines tasted more or less the same. Wine was wine. All that changed when we started to taste wine the way the pros do.

The Special Technique for Tasting Wine

We know you're out there — the cynics who are saying, right about now, "Hey, I already know how to taste. I do it every day, three to five times a day. All that wine-tasting humbug is just another way of making wine seem fancy."

And you know, in a way, those cynics are right. Anyone who can taste coffee or a hamburger can taste wine. All you need is a nose, taste buds, and a brain. You also have all that you need to speak Mandarin. However, having the *ability* to do something is different from knowing *how* to do it and applying that know-how in everyday life.

Two very complicated rules of wine tasting

You drink beverages every day, tasting them as they pass through your mouth. In the case of wine, however, drinking and tasting are not synonymous. Wine is much more complex than other beverages: More is going on in a mouthful of wine. For example, most wines have lots of different (and subtle) flavors, all at the same time, and they give you multiple sensations when they're in your mouth, such as softness and sharpness together.

If you just drink wine, gulping it down the way you do soda, you miss a lot of what you paid for. But if you *taste* wine, you can discover its nuances. In fact, the more slowly and attentively you taste wine, the more interesting the wine tastes.

Two of the fundamental rules of wine tasting are

1. Slow down.
2. Pay attention.

The appearance of the wine

We enjoy looking at the wine in our glass, noticing how brilliant the wine is and the way it reflects the light, trying to decide precisely which shade of red to call the wine and whether that particular red will stain the tablecloth permanently if we tilt the glass too far.

Most books tell you that you look at the wine to determine whether the wine is clear (because cloudiness generally indicates a flawed wine). That advice dates itself, though. Ever since high technology infiltrated the wine industry, visual flaws in wine are as rare as a winning lottery ticket. You could probably drink wine every night for a year without encountering a cloudy wine.

Look at the wine for a moment, anyway. Tilt your (half-full) glass away from you and look at the color of the wine against a white background, such as the tablecloth or a piece of paper (a colored background distorts the color of the wine). Notice how dark or how pale and what color the wine is, for the record. Eventually, you'll begin to notice differences from one wine to the next; but for now, just observe.

The nose knows

Now we get to the really fun part of tasting wine: swirling and sniffing. This is when you can let your imagination run wild, and no one will ever dare to contradict you. If you say that a wine smells like wild strawberries to you, how can anyone prove that it doesn't?

Tips for smelling wine

1. Be bold. Stick your nose right into the airspace of the glass where all the aromas are captured.
2. Don't wear a strong scent; it will compete with the smell of the wine.
3. Don't knock yourself out smelling a wine when strong food aromas are around. The tomatoes you smell in the wine could really be the tomato in someone's pasta sauce.
4. Become a smeller. Smell every ingredient when you cook, everything you eat, the fresh fruits and vegetables you buy at the supermarket, even the smells of your environment — like leather, wet earth, fresh road tar, grass, flowers, your wet dog, shoe polish, and your medicine cabinet. Stuff your mental database with smells so that you'll have aroma memories at your disposal when you need to draw on them.
5. Try different techniques of sniffing. Some people like to take short, quick sniffs, while others like to inhale a deep whiff of the wine's smell. Keeping your mouth open a bit while you inhale can help you perceive aromas. (Some people even hold one nostril closed and smell with the other, but we think that's a bit kinky, especially in family restaurants.)

Before we explain the smelling ritual, and the tasting technique that goes along with it (described in the next section), we want to assure you that (a) you don't have to apply this procedure to every single wine you drink; (b) you won't look foolish doing "it," at least in the eyes of other wine lovers (we can't speak for the other 90 percent of the human population); and (c) it's a great trick at parties to avoid talking with someone you don't like.

To get the most out of your sniffing, keep your glass on the table and rotate the glass so that the wine swirls around inside the glass and air mixes with the wine. Don't even *think* about swirling your wine if your glass is more than half full. After swirling, bring the glass to your nose quickly. Stick your nose as far as it will go into the airspace of the glass without actually touching the wine, and smell the wine. Free-associate. Is the aroma fruity, woodsy, fresh, cooked, intense, light? Your nose tires quickly, but it recovers quickly, too. Wait just a moment and try again. Listen to your friends' comments and try to find the same things they find in the aroma.

You can revitalize your nose more quickly by smelling something else, like your water, a piece of bread, or your shirt sleeve — but be prepared for the odd looks you'll get from everyone around you.

As you swirl, the aromas in the wine vaporize, and you can smell them. Wine has so many *aromatic compounds* that whatever you find in the smell of a wine is probably not merely a figment of your imagination.

Wines have noses

With poetic license typical of wine tasters, someone once dubbed the smell of a wine its *nose* — and the expression took hold. If someone says that a wine has a huge nose, he means that the wine has a very strong smell. If he says that he detects lemon *in the nose* or *on the nose,* he means that the wine smells like lemons.

In fact, most wine tasters rarely use the word *smell* to describe how a wine smells because the word *smell* (like the word *odor*) seems derogatory. Wine tasters talk about the wine's nose or aroma. Sometimes they use the word *bouquet,* although that word is falling out of fashion.

Wines have palates, too

Just as a wine taster might use the term *nose* for the smell of a wine, he might use the word *palate* in referring to the taste of a wine. A wine's palate is the overall impression the wine gives in your mouth, or any isolated aspect of the wine's taste — as in "This wine has a harmonious palate," or "The palate of this wine is a bit acidic." When a wine taster says that he finds raspberries *on the palate,* he means that the wine has the flavor of raspberries.

The point behind this whole ritual of swirling and sniffing is that what you smell should be pleasurable to you, maybe even fascinating, and that you should have fun in the process. But what if you notice a smell that you don't like?

Hang around wine geeks for a while, and you'll start to hear words like *petrol, manure, sweaty saddle, burnt match,* and *asparagus* used to describe the aromas of some wines. "Yuck!" you say? Of course you do! Fortunately, the wines that exhibit such smells are not the wines you'll be drinking for the most part — at least not unless you really catch the wine bug. And when you do catch the wine bug, you may discover that those aromas, in the right wine, can really be a kick. Even if you don't come to enjoy those smells (some of us do, honest!), you'll appreciate them as typical characteristics of certain regions or grapes.

When a wine is seriously flawed, the nose of the wine is often immediately affected. Wine judges have a term for such wines. They call them DNPIM — Do Not Put In Mouth. Not that you'll get ill, but why subject your taste buds to the same abuse that your nose just took?

The mouth action

After you've looked at the wine and smelled it, you're finally allowed to taste it.

Here's how the procedure goes. Take a medium-sized sip of wine. Hold the wine in your mouth, purse your lips, and draw in some air across your tongue, over the wine. (Be utterly

Ten aromas (or flavors) associated with wine

1. Fruits
2. Herbs
3. Vegetables
4. Earth
5. Flowers
6. Grass
7. Tobacco
8. Toast
9. Smoke
10. Coffee, mocha, or chocolate

careful not to choke or dribble, or everyone will strongly suspect that you're new at this.) Swish the wine around in your mouth as if you are chewing it. Then swallow. The whole process should take several seconds, depending on how much you're concentrating on the wine. Wondering what to concentrate on? Here's what:

- **Feeling the tastes:** Different parts of the tongue specialize in registering different sensations; sweetness is perceived most keenly on the front of the tongue, sourness is triggered principally on the sides, and bitterness is detected particularly across the rear of the tongue. By moving the wine around in your mouth, you give the wine a chance to hit all of these places.
- **Tasting the smells:** Until you cut your nose in on the action, all you can taste in the wine is the sensation of sweetness, acidity, and bitterness — plus a general impression of weight and texture. Where have all the wild strawberries gone?

  The strawberries are still in the wine, right next to the chocolate and plums. But — to be perfectly correct about it — these flavors are actually *aromas* that you taste, not through tongue contact, but by inhaling them up an interior nasal passage in the back of your mouth. When you draw in air across the wine in your mouth, you vaporize the aromas just as you did when you swirled the wine in your glass.

After you go through all this rigmarole, you're ready to reach a conclusion: Do you like what you tasted? The possible answers are yes, no, an indifferent shrug of the shoulders, or "I'm not sure, let me take another taste," which means that you have serious wine-nerd potential.

Parlez-Vous Winespeak?

We have to confess that there is one step between knowing how to taste wine and always drinking wine that you like. And it's a doozy. That step is putting taste into words so that another person can steer you in the right direction.

You have two hurdles here: Finding the words to describe what you like or don't like, and then getting the other person to understand what you mean. Naturally, it helps if we all speak the same language.

The tastes of a wine actually reveal themselves sequentially as the tongue detects them. We recommend that you follow this natural sequence when you try to put words to what you're tasting.

Unfortunately, Winespeak is a dialect with an undisciplined and sometimes poetic vocabulary whose definitions change all the time, depending on who is speaking. For now, here are a few basic words and concepts that should do the trick.

- **Sweetness:** Right on the tip of your tongue, as soon as you put the wine into your mouth, you can notice sweetness or the lack of it. In Winespeak, *dry* is the opposite of *sweet.* Classify the wine you're tasting as *dry, off-dry* (in other words, somewhat sweet), or *sweet.*

Is that sweetness or fruitiness?

Beginning wine tasters sometimes describe dry wines as sweet because they confuse fruitiness with sweetness. A wine is *fruity* when it has distinct aromas and flavors of fruit. You smell the fruitiness with your nose; in your mouth, you "smell" the fruitiness through your retronasal passage.

Sweetness, on the other hand, is a tactile impression on your tongue. When in doubt, try holding your nose when you taste the wine; if the wine really is sweet, you'll be able to taste the sweetness despite the fact that you can't smell the fruitiness.

- **Acidity:** All wine contains acid (mainly *tartaric acid,* which exists in grapes), but some wines are more acidic than others. Acidity is more of a taste factor in white wines than in reds. For white wines, acidity is the backbone of the wine's taste. White wines with a good amount of acidity taste *crisp,* and those without enough acidity taste *fat* and *flabby.* The sides of the tongue trigger your perception of acidity. You can also sense the consequences of acidity (or the lack of it) in the overall style of the wine — whether the wine is a tart little number or a soft and generous sort, for example. You can classify the wine as *tart, crisp, soft,* or "couch potato."
- **Tannin:** Tannin is a substance that exists naturally in the skins, seeds (or *pips*), and stems of grapes. Because red wines are fermented with their grape skins and pips, tannin levels are far higher in red wines than in white wines. Have you ever sipped a red wine and rapidly experienced a drying-out feeling in your mouth, as if someone had shoved a blotter in there? That's tannin.

  Tannin is to red wine what acidity is to white: a backbone. You sense tannin near the back of your tongue, but you can detect it elsewhere, too — on the inside of your cheeks and between your cheeks and gums — if the amount of tannin in a wine is high. Depending on the amount and nature of its tannin, a red wine can be called *astringent, firm,* or *soft.*

Touchy-feely

Softness and firmness are actually *textural impressions* a wine gives you as you taste it. Just as your mouth feels temperature in a liquid, your mouth also feels texture. Some wines literally *feel* soft and smooth in your mouth, while others feel hard, rough, or coarse. In white wines, acid is usually responsible for impressions of hardness or firmness (or crispness); in red wines, tannin is usually responsible. Low levels of either substance can make a wine feel pleasantly soft — or too soft, depending on the wine and your taste preferences. Unfermented sugar also contributes to an impression of softness, and alcohol can, too. But very high alcohol — which is fairly common in wines these days — can give a wine an edge of hardness.

Is it acid or tannin?

Red wines have acid as well as tannin, and distinguishing between the two as you taste a wine can be a real challenge. When you're not sure whether you're perceiving mainly tannin or acid, pay attention to how your mouth feels *after* you've swallowed the wine. Both tannin and acid will make your mouth feel dry, but acid makes you salivate in response to the dry feeling (saliva is alkaline and neutralizes the acid). Tannin just leaves your mouth dry.

- **Body:** A wine's body is an impression you get from the whole of the wine — not at any one place on your tongue. It's the impression of the weight and size of the wine in your mouth, which is usually attributable principally to a wine's alcohol. We say "impression" because, obviously, one ounce of any wine will occupy exactly the same space in your mouth and weigh the same as one ounce of any other wine. But some wines *seem* fuller, bigger, or heavier in the mouth than others. Think about the wine's fullness and weight as you taste it. Don't tell your friends that you're doing this, but imagine that your tongue is a tiny postal scale and judge how much the wine weighs it down. Classify the wine as *light-bodied, medium-bodied,* or *full-bodied.*
- **Flavors:** Wines have flavors (er, we mean *mouth aromas*), but wines don't come *in* a specific flavor. Although you may enjoy the suggestion of chocolate in a red wine that you're tasting, you wouldn't want to go to a wine store and ask for a chocolatey wine — unless you don't mind the idea of people holding their hands over their mouths and trying not to laugh aloud at you.

In wine, you want to refer to *families of flavors.* You have your *fruity wines* (the ones that make you think of all sorts of fruit when you smell them or hold the wine in your mouth), your *earthy wines* (these make you think of mushrooms, walks in the forest, turning the earth in your garden, dry leaves, and so on), your *spicy wines* (cinnamon, cloves, black pepper, or Indian spices, for example), your *herbal wines* (mint, grass, hay, rosemary, and so on), and so on, and so on. Wine has so many flavors that we could go on and on (and we often do!), but you get the picture, right?

If you like a wine and want to try another wine that's similar but different (and the wine will always be different, we guarantee you), one method is to decide what families of flavors you like in the wine and mention that to the person selling you your next bottle.

Now you have 13 words — and a whole community of families — that allow you to explain what kind of wine you like. (If you're superstitious, consider *couch* and *potato* as separate words, and you have 14.)

The Quality Issue

Did you notice, by any chance, that nowhere in the list of terms we use to describe wines are the words *great, very good,* or *good?* Instead of worrying about crisp wines, earthy wines, and medium-bodied wines, wouldn't it just be easier to walk into a wine shop and say, "Give me a very good wine for dinner tonight"? Isn't *quality* the ultimate issue — or at least, quality within your price range, also known as *value?*

Well, quality is so important that (our cats will tell you with some embarrassment) we sometimes argue at the dinner table about the quality of the wine we're drinking. It's not that we don't know a great wine when we find one; in fact, we usually agree on whether the wine we are drinking is good. What we debate is *how* good the wine is or isn't — because *how* good is a matter of personal taste.

The instruments that measure the quality of a wine are a human being's nose and mouth, and because we're all different, we all have different opinions on how good a wine is.

So, what's a good wine? A good wine is, above all, a wine that you like enough to drink. After that, how good a wine is depends on how that wine measures up to a set of (more or less) agreed-upon standards of performance established by experienced, trained experts. These standards involve such mysterious concepts as *balance, length, depth, complexity, finish,* and *trueness to type* (*typicity* in Winespeak, *typicité* in

Snobwinespeak). None of these concepts are objectively measurable, by the way.

- **Balance:** Three words we talk about in the "Parlez-Vous Winespeak?" section in this chapter — sweetness, acidity, and tannin — represent three of the major *components* (parts) of wine. The fourth is alcohol. Besides being one of the reasons we usually want to drink a glass of wine in the first place, alcohol is an important element of wine quality.

  Balance is the relationship of these four components to one another. A wine is balanced when nothing sticks out as you taste it, like harsh tannin or too much sweetness. Most wines are balanced to most people. But if you have any pet peeves about food — if you really hate anything tart, for example, or if you never eat sweets — you might perceive some wines to be unbalanced. If you perceive a wine to be unbalanced, then that wine *is* unbalanced for you. (Professional tasters know their own idiosyncrasies and adjust for them when they judge wine.)

  Tannin and acidity are *hardening elements* in a wine (they make a wine taste firmer in the mouth), whereas alcohol and sugar (if any) are *softening elements.* The balance of a wine is the interrelationship of the hard and the soft aspects of a wine, and a key indicator of quality.

- **Length:** When we call wines *long* or *short,* we're not referring to the size of the bottle or how quickly we empty it. *Length* is a word used to describe a wine that goes all the way on the palate — you can taste it across the full length of your tongue — and doesn't stop short halfway through your tasting. A wine with good length hits all the taste centers on your tongue. Many wines today are very up-front on the palate — they make a big impression as soon as you taste them — but they are short. Length is a sure sign of quality.

- **Depth:** This is another subjective, unmeasurable attribute of a high-quality wine. We say a wine has *depth* when it doesn't taste flat and one-dimensional in your mouth but instead seems to have underlying layers of taste. A flat wine can never be great.

- **Complexity:** Nothing is wrong with a simple, straightforward wine any more than something is wrong with Homer Simpson — both are just what they are. But a wine that keeps revealing different things about itself, always showing you a new flavor or impression — a wine that has *complexity* — is usually considered better quality. Some experts use the term *complexity* specifically to indicate that a wine has a multiplicity of aromas and flavors, while others use the term in a more holistic sense, to refer to the total impression a wine gives you.

- **Finish:** The impression a wine leaves in the back of your mouth and in your throat after you swallow it is its *finish* or *aftertaste.* In a good wine, you can still perceive the wine's flavors — such as fruitiness or spiciness — at that point. Some wines may finish *hot,* because of high alcohol, or *bitter,* because of tannin — both are shortcomings.
- **Typicity:** In order to judge whether a wine is true to its type, you have to know how that type is supposed to be. So you have to know the textbook characteristics of wines made from the major grape varieties and wines of the world's classic wine regions. (For example, the Cabernet Sauvignon grape typically has an aroma and flavor of blackcurrants, and the French white wine called Pouilly-Fumé typically has a slight gunflint aroma.)

Balance in action

For firsthand experience of how the principle of taste balance works, try this. Make a very strong cup of tea. When you sip it, the tea will taste bitter, because tea is very tannic. Now add lemon juice; the tea will taste astringent (constricting and drying out your mouth), because the acid of the lemon and the tannin of the tea are accentuating each other. Now add lots of sugar to the tea. The sweetness should counter-balance the acid–tannin impact, and the tea will taste softer than it did before.

Chapter 3

Pinot Envy and Other Secrets about Grape Varieties

In This Chapter

- Descriptions of major grape varieties and their wines
- Genus, species, variety, and other grape terms

We love to visit wine country — which for us means "anywhere in the world where vineyards are." Gazing across manicured rows of grapevines in Napa Valley or pondering craggy terraces of rugged vines on the hillsides of Portugal inspires us — and reinforces for us the fact that wine is an agricultural product, born of the earth, the grapevine, and the hard work of humans. Literally and emotionally, grapes are the link between the land and the wine.

Grapes also happen to give us one of the easiest ways of classifying wine and making sense of the hundreds of different types of wine that exist.

It's the Grape Whodunit

If anyone were to invent a mystery game about wine, the game would probably be a big flop because knowing what makes most wines taste the way they do is no real mystery. The grapes done it! With Mother Nature and a winemaker as accomplices, the grapes are responsible for the style and personality of every wine, and sometimes the quality, because the grapes are the starting point of the wine. The grapes dictate the genetic structure of a wine and how the wine will respond to everything that's done to it.

Think back to the last wine you drank. What color was it? If the wine was white, the odds are that it came from the family of white grapes; if the wine was pink or red, that's because the wine came from red grapes. Did the wine smell herbal or earthy or fruity? Whichever, those aromas came from the grapes. Was the wine firm and tannic or soft and voluptuous? Thank the grapes (with a nod to their co-conspirators, Nature and the winemaker).

The specific grape variety (or varieties) that makes any given wine is largely responsible for the sensory characteristics the wine offers — from appearance, to aromas, flavors, and its alcohol–tannin–acid profile.

Of genus and species

By *grape variety,* we mean the fruit of a specific type of grapevine: the fruit of the Cabernet Sauvignon vine, for example, or of the Chardonnay vine.

The term *variety* actually has specific meaning in scientific circles. A variety is a subdivision of a species. Most of the world's wines are made from grape varieties that belong to the species *vinifera* — itself a subdivision of the genus *Vitis.* This species originated in Europe and western Asia; other distinct species of *Vitis* are native to North America. Grapes of other species can also make wine — such as the Concord grape of the native American species *Vitis labrusca,* which makes Concord wine as well as grape juice and jelly.

How the grape done it

All sorts of attributes distinguish each grape variety from the next. These attributes fall into two categories: personality traits and performance factors. Both types of characteristics affect the ultimate taste and style of wines made from a specific grape variety.

Personality traits of grape varieties

Personality traits are the characteristics of the fruit itself — its flavors, for example.

Skin color is the most fundamental distinction among grape varieties. Every grape variety is considered either a white variety or a red (or "black") one, according to the color of its skins when the grapes are ripe. Individual grape varieties also differ from one another in other ways.

- **Aromatic compounds:** Some grapes (like Muscat) contribute floral aromas and flavors to their wine, for example, while other grapes contribute herbaceous notes (as Sauvignon Blanc does) or fruity character. Some grapes have very neutral aromas and flavors and, therefore, make fairly neutral wines.
- **Acidity levels:** Some grapes are naturally disposed to higher acid levels than others, which influences the wine made from those grapes.
- **Thickness of skin and size of the individual grapes (called *berries*):** Black grapes with thick skins naturally have more tannin than grapes with thin skins; ditto for small-berried varieties compared to large-berried varieties, because their skin-to-juice ratio is higher. More tannin translates into a firmer, more tannic red wine.

The composite personality traits of any grape variety are fairly evident in wines made from that grape. A Cabernet Sauvignon wine is almost always more tannic and slightly lower in alcohol than a Merlot wine, for example, because that's the nature of those two grapes.

Performance factors of grape varieties

Performance factors refer to how the grapevine grows, how its fruit ripens, and how quickly it can get from 0 to 60 miles per hour. The performance factors that distinguish grape varieties are vitally important to the grape grower because those factors determine how easy or challenging it will be for the grower to cultivate a specific variety in his vineyard — if he can grow it at all. The issues include

- How much time a variety typically needs to ripen its grapes. (In regions with short summers, early-ripening varieties do best.)

- How dense and compact the bunches of grapes are. (In warm, damp climates, grape varieties with dense bunches can have mildew problems.)
- How much vegetation a particular variety tends to grow. (In fertile soils, a vine that's disposed to grow lots of leaves and shoots could have so much vegetation that the grapes don't get enough sun to ripen.)

The reasons some grape varieties perform brilliantly in certain places (and make excellent wine as a result) are so complex that grape growers haven't figured them all out yet. The amount of heat and cold, the amount of wind and rain (or lack of it), and the slant of the sun's rays on a hillside of vines are among the factors affecting a vine's performance. In any case, no two vineyards in the world have precisely the same combination of these factors — precisely the same *terroir* (see Chapter 4). The issue simply defies simple generalizations.

A Primer on White Grape Varieties

This section includes descriptions of the 12 most important white *vinifera* varieties today. In describing the grapes, naturally we describe the types of wine that are made from each grape. These wines could be varietal wines, or place-name wines that don't mention the grape variety anywhere on the label (a common practice for European wines; see Chapter 4). These grapes could also be blending partners for other grapes, in wines made from multiple grape varieties. (Turn to Chapter 2 for a quick review of some of the descriptors we use in this section.)

Chardonnay

Today's darling white grape, Chardonnay, is quite a regal grape, producing the greatest dry white wines in the world — white Burgundies. Chardonnay is also one of the main grapes of Champagne. The Chardonnay grape grows in practically every wine-producing country of the world, for two reasons: It's relatively adaptable, and the name Chardonnay on a wine label is a sure-fire sales tool.

Because the flavors of Chardonnay are very compatible with those of oak — and because white Burgundy (the great prototype) is generally an oaked wine, and because many wine drinkers love the flavor of oak — most Chardonnay wine receives some oak treatment either during or after fermentation. Chardonnay itself has fruity aromas and flavors that range from apple — in cooler wine regions — to tropical fruits, especially pineapple, in warmer regions. Chardonnay also can display subtle earthy aromas, such as mushroom or minerals. Chardonnay wine has medium-to-high acidity and is generally full-bodied. Classically, Chardonnay wines are dry. However, most inexpensive Chardonnays these days are actually a bit sweet.

Chardonnay is a grape that can stand on its own in a wine, and the top Chardonnay-based wines (except for Champagne and similar bubblies) are 100 percent Chardonnay. But less expensive wines that are labeled *Chardonnay* — those selling for less than $8 a bottle in the U.S., for example — are likely to have some other, far less distinguished grape blended in. That's because blending in wine from an ordinary grape like Colombard helps reduce the cost of making the wine. Anyway, it's perfectly legal. And who can even tell if it's all Chardonnay or not, behind all that oak?

Riesling

The great Riesling wines of Germany have put the Riesling grape on the charts as an undisputedly noble variety. Riesling shows its real class only in a few places outside of Germany, however. The Alsace region of France, Austria, and the Finger Lakes district of New York are among the few.

Riesling wines are as unpopular today as Chardonnay is popular. Maybe that's because Riesling is the antithesis of Chardonnay. While Chardonnay is usually gussied up with oak, Riesling never is; while Chardonnay can be full-bodied and rich, Riesling is more often light-bodied and refreshing. Riesling's fresh, vivid personality can make many Chardonnays taste clumsy in comparison.

The common perception of Riesling wines is that they are sweet, and many of them are — but plenty of them aren't. Alsace Rieslings are normally dry, many German Rieslings are dry, and a few American Rieslings are dry. (Riesling can be vinified either way, according to the style of wine a producer wants to make.) Look for the word *trocken* (meaning dry) on German Riesling labels and the word *dry* on American labels if you prefer the dry style of Riesling.

High acidity, low-to-medium alcohol levels, and aromas/flavors that range from ebulliently fruity to flowery to minerally are trademarks of Riesling.

Sauvignon Blanc

While just about everybody likes Chardonnay, Sauvignon Blanc is controversial with wine drinkers. That's because it has such distinctive character.

For one thing, Sauvignon Blanc is high in acidity — great if you like crisp wines, but not so great otherwise. For another thing, its aromas and flavors can be herbaceous (suggestive of herbs or grass) — delicious and intriguing to some wine lovers, but too weird for others.

Sauvignon Blanc wines are light-bodied to medium-bodied and usually dry. European versions are unoaked more often than oaked, but in California the wines can be oaky and not fully dry — in the Chardonnay-wannabe style. Besides herbaceous character (sometimes referred to as *grassy*), Sauvignon Blanc wines display mineral aromas and flavors, vegetal character, or — in certain climates — fruity character, such as ripe melon, figs, or passion fruit.

Pinot Gris/Pinot Grigio

Pinot Gris (*gree*) is one of several grape varieties called *Pinot:* There's Pinot Blanc (white Pinot), Pinot Noir (black Pinot), Pinot Meunier (we don't know how that one translates), and Pinot Gris (gray Pinot), which is called *Pinot Grigio* in Italian. Pinot Gris is believed to have mutated from the black Pinot Noir grape. Although the grape is considered white, its skin color is unusually dark for a white variety.

Wines made from Pinot Gris can be deeper in color than most white wines — although Italy's Pinot Grigio wines are quite pale. Pinot Gris wines are medium- to full-bodied, with rather low acidity and fairly neutral aromas. Sometimes the flavor and aroma can suggest the skins of fruit, such as peach skins or orange rind.

Other white grapes

Table 3-1 describes some other grapes whose names you see on wine labels, or whose wine you could drink in place-name wines without realizing it.

Table 3-1 Other White Grapes and Their Characteristics

Grape Type	*Characteristics*
Albariño	An aromatic grape from the northwestern corner of Spain — the wine region called Rias Baixas — and Portugal's northerly Vinho Verde region, where it's called *Alvarinho.* It makes medium-bodied, crisp, unoaked, appley-tasting white wines whose high glycerine gives them silky texture.
Chenin Blanc	A noble grape in the Loire Valley of France, for Vouvray and other wines. The best wines have high acidity and a fascinating oily texture (they feel rather viscous in your mouth). Some good dry Chenin Blanc comes from California, but so does a ton of ordinary off-dry wine. In South Africa, Chenin Blanc is often called *Steen.*
Gewürztraminer *(geh-VAIRTZ-trah-mee-ner)*	A wonderfully exotic grape that makes fairly deep-colored, full-bodied, soft white wines with aromas and flavors of roses and lychee fruit. France's Alsace region is the classic domain of this variety; the wines have pronounced floral and fruity aromas and flavors, but are actually dry — as fascinating as they are delicious. The most commercial style of U.S. Gewürztraminer is light, sweetish, and relatively insipid, but a few wineries in California, Oregon, and New York do make good, dry Gewürztraminer.

(continued)

Table 3-1 *(continued)*

Grape Type	*Characteristics*
Grüner Veltliner	A native Austrian variety that boasts complex aromas and flavors (vegetal, spicy, mineral), rich texture, and usually substantial weight.
Muscat	An aromatic grape that makes Italy's sparkling Asti (which, incidentally, tastes *exactly* like ripe Muscat grapes). Extremely pretty floral aromas. In Alsace and Austria, makes a dry wine, and in lots of places (southern France, southern Italy, Australia) makes a delicious, sweet dessert wine through the addition of alcohol.
Pinot Blanc	Fairly neutral in aroma and flavors, yet can make characterful wines. High acidity and low sugar levels translate into dry, crisp, medium-bodied wines. Alsace, Austria, northern Italy, and Germany are the main production zones.
Sémillon *(seh-mee-yohn)*	Sauvignon Blanc's classic blending partner and a good grape in its own right. Sémillon wine is relatively low in acid (compared to Sauvignon Blanc, anyway) and has attractive but subtle aromas — lanolin sometimes, although it can be slightly herbaceous when young. A major grape in Australia, and southwestern France, including Bordeaux (where it is the key player in Sauternes).
Viognier *(vee-ohn-yay)*	A grape from France's Rhône Valley that's becoming popular in California and the south of France. With a floral aroma, delicately apricot-like, medium- to full-bodied with low acidity.

A Primer on Red Grape Varieties

Here are descriptions of 12 important red vinifera grape varieties. You'll encounter these grapes in varietal wines and also in place-name wines. See Chapter 4 for a chart listing the grape varieties of major place-name wines.

Cabernet Sauvignon

Cabernet Sauvignon is not only a noble grape variety but also an adaptable one, growing well in just about any climate that isn't very cool. The Cabernet Sauvignon grape makes wines that are high in tannin and are medium- to full-bodied. The textbook descriptor for Cabernet Sauvignon's aroma and flavor is *blackcurrants* or *cassis;* the grape can also contribute vegetal tones to a wine when or where the grapes are less than ideally ripe.

Like Chardonnay, Cabernet Sauvignon grows well in many different wine regions. As a result, Cabernet Sauvignon wines come in all price and quality levels, from numerous countries. The least-expensive versions are usually quite soft and nondescriptly fruity (not specifically blackcurrants), with medium body at best. The best wines are rich and firm with great depth and classic Cabernet flavor. Serious Cabernet Sauvignons can age for 15 years or more.

Because Cabernet Sauvignon is fairly tannic (and because of the blending precedent in Bordeaux), the wine is often blended with other grapes; Merlot — being less tannic — usually is considered an ideal partner. However, Australian winemakers have the unusual practice of blending Cabernet Sauvignon with Syrah.

Cabernet Sauvignon often goes by just its first name, Cabernet (although there are other Cabernets) or even by its nickname, *Cab.*

Merlot

Deep color, full body, high alcohol, and low tannin are the characteristics of wines made from the Merlot grape. The aromas and flavors can be plummy or sometimes chocolatey, or they can suggest tea leaves.

Some wine drinkers find Merlot easier to like than Cabernet Sauvignon because it's less tannic. (But some winemakers feel that Merlot is not satisfactory in its own right, and thus often blend Merlot with Cabernet Sauvignon, Cabernet Franc, or both.)

Pinot Noir

The late Andre Tchelitscheff, the legendary winemaker of some of California's finest Cabernets, once told us that if he could do it all over again, he'd make Pinot Noir instead of Cab. He's probably not alone. Pinot Noir is finicky, troublesome, enigmatic, and challenging. But a great Pinot Noir can be one of the greatest wines ever.

Pinot Noir wine is lighter in color than Cabernet or Merlot. It has relatively high alcohol, medium-to-high acidity, and medium-to-low tannin (although oak barrels can contribute additional tannin to the wine). Pinot Noir's flavors and aromas can be very fruity — often like a mélange of red berries — or earthy and woodsy, depending on how the grape is grown and/or vinified. Pinot Noir is rarely blended with other grapes.

Syrah/Shiraz

Syrah produces deeply colored wines with full body, firm tannin, and aromas/flavors that can suggest berries, smoked meat, bell peppers, spice, tar, or even burnt rubber (believe it or not). In Australia, Syrah (called Shiraz) comes in several styles — some of them charming, medium-bodied wines with strawberry-like flavor that are quite the opposite of the Northern Rhône's powerful Syrahs.

Syrah doesn't require any other grape to complement its flavors, although in Australia it is often blended with Cabernet. In the Southern Rhône, Syrah is often part of a blended wine with Grenache and other varieties.

Zinfandel

White Zinfandel is such a popular wine — and so much better known than the red style of Zinfandel — that its fans might argue that Zinfandel is a white grape. But it's really red.

Zin — as lovers of red Zinfandel call it — makes rich, dark wines that are high in alcohol and medium to high in tannin. The wines can have a blackberry or raspberry aroma and flavor, a spicy character, or even a jammy flavor. Some Zins are lighter than others and meant to be enjoyed young, and some are serious wines with a tannin structure that's built for aging. (You can tell which is which by the price.)

Nebbiolo

Outside of scattered sites in Northwestern Italy — mainly the Piedmont region — Nebbiolo just doesn't make remarkable wine. But the extraordinary quality of Barolo and Barbaresco, two Piedmont wines, prove what greatness it can achieve under the right conditions.

The Nebbiolo grape is high in both tannin and acid, which can make a wine tough. Fortunately, the grape also gives enough alcohol to soften the package. Its color can be deep when the wine is young but can develop orangey tinges within a few years. The wine's complex aroma is fruity (strawberry and jam), earthy and woodsy (tar, truffles), herbal (mint, eucalyptus, anise), and floral (roses).

Lighter versions of Nebbiolo are meant to be drunk young — wines labeled Nebbiolo d'Alba, Roero, or Nebbiolo delle Langhe, for example — while Barolo and Barbaresco are wines that really deserve a *minimum* of eight years' age before drinking.

Sangiovese

This Italian grape has proven itself in the Tuscany region of Italy, especially in the Brunello di Montalcino and Chianti districts, and is increasingly popular in California. Sangiovese makes wines that are medium to high in acidity and firm in tannin; the wines can be light-bodied to full-bodied, depending on exactly where the grapes grow and how the wine is made. The aromas and flavors of the wines are fruity — especially cherry, often tart cherry — with floral nuances of violets and sometimes a slightly nutty character.

Tempranillo

Tempranillo is Spain's candidate for greatness. This grape gives wines deep color, low acidity, and only moderate alcohol. Modern renditions of Tempranillo prove what color and fruitiness this grape has. In more traditional wines, much of the grape's color and flavor is lost due to long wood aging and to blending with varieties that lack color, such as Grenache.

Other red grapes

Table 3-2 describes additional red grape varieties and their wines, which you could encounter either as varietal wines or as wines named for their place of production.

Table 3-2 Other Red Grapes and Their Characteristics

Grape Type	*Characteristics*
Aglianico	Little known outside Southern Italy, it makes age-worthy, powerful red wines, high in tannin.
Barbera	Italian variety that, oddly for a red grape, has little tannin but very high acidity. When fully ripe, it can give big, fruity wines with refreshing crispness.
Cabernet Franc	A parent of Cabernet Sauvignon, and often blended with it to make Bordeaux-style wines. Ripens earlier, has more expressive, fruitier flavor and less tannin. A specialty of the Loire Valley in France.
Gamay	Excels in the Beaujolais district of France. Gamay makes grapey wines that can be low in tannin — although the Gamay grape itself is fairly tannic. Neither *Gamay Beaujolais* in California nor *Napa Gamay* is true Gamay.
Grenache	A Spanish grape by origin, called Garnacha there. (Most wine drinkers associate Grenache with France's southern Rhône Valley more than with Spain, however.) In the right circumstances, it can make deeply colored wines with velvety texture and flavors suggestive of raspberries.

Chapter 4

Is It a Grape? Is It a Place?

In This Chapter

- A quick trick to decoding wine names
- The myth of varietal wines
- The secret cult of *terroir*
- Branded wines, generics, and proprietary names

We remember a cartoon in *The New Yorker* some years ago that depicted the students of a private nursery school lined up for their class picture. The caption identified the children only by their first names. Every girl was Jennifer, and every boy was Scott.

When you walk into a wine shop these days, you'd think that the people who name wines have the same fixation as the parents of those nursery school children. More than half the white wines are named *Chardonnay,* and the majority of the red wines are named either *Cabernet Sauvignon* or *Merlot.*

Actually, one Merlot is no more identical to the next than one little Jennifer is identical to the next. But to distinguish one Merlot from the other (without opening the bottles, that is), you need more information. You need to read the rest of the label.

What's in a Name

All sorts of names can appear on wine labels. These names often include

- The name of the *grape* from which the wine was made.
- A *brand name,* which is often the name of the company or person that made the wine (who is called the *producer*).
- Sometimes a special, invented name for that particular wine (called a *proprietary name*).
- The name of the *place,* or *places,* where the grapes grew (the wine region, and sometimes the name of the specific vineyard property).

Then there's the *vintage* year (the year the grapes were harvested), which is part of the wine's identity; and sometimes you see a descriptor like *reserve,* which either has specific legal meaning or means nothing at all, depending on where the wine came from.

Veteran wine lovers appreciate all this detailed information on wine labels because they know how to interpret it. But to anyone who is just discovering wine, the information embedded in wine names is more confusing than enlightening. Although we'd all agree that little Jennifer needs more than just the name *Jennifer* to identify herself in the world (unless she plans to become a rock star or comedienne), does she really need the equivalent of: Jennifer Smith, "Jenny," Caucasian female, upper middle class, produced by Don and Louise Smith, New York City, Upper West Side, 1995?

Of course she doesn't. But — we know you don't want to hear this — for bottles of wine the answer, frankly, is yes.

The Wine Name Game

Most of the wines that you find in your wine shop or on restaurant wine lists are named in one of two basic ways: either for their *grape variety* or for the *place where the grapes grew.* That information, plus the name of the producer, becomes the shorthand name we use in talking about the wine.

Robert Mondavi Cabernet Sauvignon, for example, is a wine made by Robert Mondavi Winery and named after the Cabernet Sauvignon grape. Fontodi Chianti Classico is a wine made by the Fontodi winery and named after the place called Chianti Classico.

You might recognize some names as grape names (refer to Chapter 3) and other names as place-names right off the bat; but if you don't, don't panic. That information is the kind of thing you can look up.

Hello, my name is Chardonnay

A *varietal* wine is a wine that is named after either the *principal* or the *sole* grape variety that makes up the wine.

Each country (and in the U.S., some individual states) has laws that dictate the minimum percentage of the named grape that a wine must contain if that wine wants to call itself by a grape name. The issue is truth in advertising.

U.S. federal regulations fix the legal minimum percentage of the named grape at 75 percent (which means that your favorite California Chardonnay could contain as much as 25 percent of some *other* grape). In Oregon, the minimum is 90 percent (except for Cabernet, which can be 75 percent). In Australia, it's 85 percent. And in the countries that form the European Union (EU), the minimum is 85 percent.

Some varietal wines are made *entirely* from the grape variety for which the wine is named. There's no law against that anywhere.

Most of the time, the labels of varietal wines don't tell you whether other grapes are present in the wine, what those grapes are, or the percentage of the wine that they account for. You can only know that the wine contains at least the minimum legal percentage of the named variety. Interestingly, if a wine is named for two or more grape varieties — say that the wine is a Semillon-Chardonnay, for example — the label must state the percentages of each, and these percentages must total 100 percent. Now that's an honest varietal wine!

Most California (and other American) wines carry varietal names. Likewise, most Australian, South American, and South African wines are named using the *principal* principle. Even some countries that don't normally name their wines after grapes, like France, are jumping on the varietal-name bandwagon for certain wines that they especially want to sell to Americans.

A common perception among some wine lovers is that a varietal wine is somehow *better* than a non-varietal wine. Actually, the fact that a wine is named after its principal grape variety is absolutely *no indication of quality.*

Hello, my name is Bordeaux

Unlike American wines, most European wines are named for the *region* (place) where their grapes grow rather than for the grape variety itself. Many of these European wines are made from precisely the same grape varieties as American wines (like Chardonnay, Cabernet Sauvignon, Sauvignon Blanc, and so on), but they don't say so on the label. Instead, the labels say Burgundy, Bordeaux, Sancerre, and so on: the *place* where those grapes grow.

Is this some nefarious plot to make wine incomprehensible to English-only wine lovers who have never visited Europe and flunked geography in school?

Au contraire! The European system of naming wines is actually intended to provide more information about each wine, and more understanding of what's in the bottle, than varietal naming does. The only catch is that to harvest this information, you have to learn something about the different regions from which the wines come.

Why name a wine after a place?

Grapes, the raw material of wine, have to grow somewhere. Depending on the type of soil, the amount of sunshine, the amount of rain, the slope of the hill, and the many other characteristics that each *somewhere* has, the grapes will turn out differently. If the grapes are different, the wine is different. Each wine, therefore, reflects the place where its grapes grow.

The same type of grape, such as Chardonnay, can get riper in one place than another. (The riper grapes make a wine higher in alcohol with riper fruit flavors.) Or the grapes (and wine) can have some subtle, unusual flavors — such as mineral flavors — attributable to a particular place. In one way or another, the place *always* affects the character of the grapes.

Decoding common European place-names

Wine Name	*Country*	*Grape Varieties*
Beaujolais	France	Gamay
Bordeaux (red)	France	Cabernet Sauvignon, Merlot, Cabernet Franc, and others*
Bordeaux (white)	France	Sauvignon Blanc, Sémillon, Muscadelle*
Burgundy (red)	France	Pinot Noir
Burgundy (white)	France	Chardonnay
Chablis	France	Chardonnay
Champagne	France	Chardonnay, Pinot Noir, Pinot Meunier*
Châteauneuf-du-Pape*	France	Grenache, Mourvèdre, Syrah, and others*
Chianti	Italy	Sangiovese, Canaiolo, and others*
Côtes du Rhône*	France	Grenache, Mourvèdre, Carignan, and others*
Port (Porto)	Portugal	Touriga Nacional, Tinta Barroca, Touriga Francesa, Tinta Roriz, Tinto Cão, and others*
Pouilly-Fuissé,	France	Chardonnay Macon, Saint Veran
Rioja (red)	Spain	Tempranillo, Grenache, and others*
Sancerre/	France	Sauvignon Blanc Pouilly-Fumé
Sauternes	France	Sémillon, Sauvignon Blanc*
Sherry	Spain	Palomino
Soave	Italy	Garganega and others*
Valpolicella	Italy	Corvina, Molinara, Rondinella*

**Indicates that a blend of grapes is used to make these wines.*

In Europe, grape growers/winemakers have had centuries to figure out which grapes grow best where. They've identified most of these grape location match-ups and codified them into wine laws. Therefore, the name of a *place* where grapes are grown in Europe automatically connotes the grape (or grapes) used to make the wine of that place. The label on the bottle usually doesn't tell you the grape (or grapes), though. Which brings us back to our original question: Is this some kind of nefarious plot to make wine incomprehensible to non-Europeans?

The terroir name game

Terroir (pronounced *ter wahr*) is based on the French word *terre,* which means soil. *Terroir* has no direct translation in English and no fixed definition, so wine people just use the French word, for expediency (not for snobbery). *Terroir* is a concept, and, like most concepts, people tend to define it more broadly or more narrowly to suit their own needs; for example, some people define *terroir* as simply dirt (as in American dirt or French dirt — it's still just dirt).

Terroir is really much more complex (and complicated) than "just dirt." *Terroir* is the combination of immutable natural factors — such as topsoil, subsoil, climate (sun, rain, wind, and so on), the slope of the hill, and altitude — that a particular vineyard site has. Chances are that no two vineyards in the entire world have precisely the same combination of these factors. So we consider *terroir* to be the *unique* combination of natural factors that a particular vineyard site has.

Terroir is the guiding principle behind the European concept that wines should be named after the place they come from (thought we'd gotten off the track, didn't you?). The thinking goes like this: The name of the place connotes which grapes were used to make the wine of that place (because the grapes are dictated by law), and the place influences the character of those grapes in its own unique way. Therefore, the most accurate name that a wine can have is the name of the place where its grapes grew.

Note: It's not some nefarious plot; it's just a whole different way of looking at things.

Place-names on American wine labels

France may have invented the concept that wines should be named after their place of origin, but neither France nor even greater Europe has a monopoly on the idea. Wine labels from non-European countries also tell you where a wine is made — usually by featuring the name of a place (called an *appellation of origin* in Winespeak) somewhere on the label. But there are a few differences between the European and non-European systems.

First of all, on an American wine label (or an Australian or Chilean or South African label, for that matter) you have to go to some effort to find the place-name on the label. The place of origin is not the fundamental name of the wine (as it is for most European wines); the grape usually is.

Second, place-names in the U.S. mean far less than they do in Europe. Okay, if the label says Napa Valley, and you've visited that area and you'd like to spend the rest of your life in one of those houses atop a hill off the Silverado Trail, Napa Valley will mean something to you. But *legally,* the name Napa Valley only means that at least 85 percent of the grapes came from an area defined by law as the Napa Valley wine zone. The name Napa Valley does not define the type of wine, nor does it imply specific grape varieties, the way a European place-name does. (Good thing the grape name is there, as big as day, on the label.)

Place-names on labels of non-European wines, for the most part, merely pay lip service to the concept of *terroir.* In fact, some non-European appellations are ridiculously broad. We have to laugh when we think how European winemakers must react to all those wine labels that announce a wine's place of origin simply as "California." *Great. This label says that this wine comes from a specific area that is 30 percent larger than the entire country of Italy! Some specific area!* (Italy has more than 300 specific wine zones.)

When the place on the label is merely *California,* in fact, that information tells you next to nothing about where the grapes grew. California's a big place, and those grapes could come from just about anywhere. Same thing for all those Australian wines labeled *South Eastern Australia* — an area only slightly smaller than France and Spain *combined.*

Wines named in other ways

Now and then, you may come across a wine that is named for neither its grape variety nor its region of origin. Such wines usually fall into three categories: *branded wines, wines with proprietary names,* or *generic wines.*

Branded wines

Most wines have brand names, including those wines that are named after their grape variety — like Simi (brand name) Sauvignon Blanc (grape) — and those that are named after their region of origin — like Masi (brand name) Valpolicella (place). These brand names are usually the name of the company that made the wine, called a *winery.* Because most wineries make several different wines, the brand name itself is not specific enough to be the actual name of the wine.

But sometimes a wine has *only* a brand name. For example, the label says *Salamandre* and *red French wine* but provides little other identification.

Grape names on European wines

Although most European wines are named after their place of origin, grape names do sometimes appear on labels of European wines.

In Italy, for example, several place-names routinely have grape names appended to them — the name Trentino (place) Pinot Grigio (grape) is an example. Or the official name of a wine could be a combination of place and grape — like the name Barbera d'Alba, which translates as Barbera (grape) of Alba (place).

In France, some producers have deliberately added the grape name to their labels even though the grape is already implicit in the wine name. For example, a white Bourgogne (place-name) might also have the word Chardonnay (grape) on the label, for those wine drinkers who don't know that white Bourgogne is 100 percent Chardonnay. And German wines usually carry grape names along with their official place-names.

But even if a European wine does carry a grape name, the most important part of the wine's name, in the eyes of the people who make the wine, is the place.

Wines that display *only* a brand name, with no indication of grape or of place — other than the country of production — are generally the most inexpensive, ordinary wines you can get. If they're from a European Union country, they won't even be *vintage dated* (that is, there won't be any indication of what year the grapes were harvested) because EU law does not entitle such wines to carry a vintage date.

Wines with proprietary names

You can find some pretty creative names on wine bottles these days: Tapestry, Conundrum, Insignia, Isosceles, Mythology, Trilogy. Is this stuff to drink, to drive, or to dab behind your ears?

Names like these are *proprietary names* (often trademarked) that producers create for special wines. In the case of American wines, the bottles with proprietary names usually contain wines made from a *blend* of grapes; therefore, no one grape name can be used as the name of the wine. (Remember California's 75 percent policy?) In the case of European wines, the grapes used to make the wine were probably not the approved grapes for that region; therefore, the regional name could not be used on the label.

Although a brand name can apply to several different wines, a proprietary name usually applies to one specific wine. You can find Zinfandel, Cabernet Sauvignon, Chardonnay, and numerous other wines under the Fetzer brand from California, for example, and you can find Beaujolais, Pouilly-Fuissé, Mâcon-Villages, and numerous other wines under the Louis Jadot brand from France. But the proprietary name Luce applies to a single wine.

A producer who creates a wine with a proprietary name has high-minded motives. He is driven by artistic impulse, intellectual curiosity, or sheer ego to form a wine that surpasses the norm for his part of the world. The price tag on the bottle reflects the magnitude of his endeavor.

Wines with proprietary names usually are made in small quantities, are quite expensive ($30 to $75 or more a bottle), and are, in fact, high in quality. They particularly satisfy wine lovers who enjoy discovering new and unusual wines. Sometimes they draw rave reviews from the critics and end up as established successes that endure in the marketplace. Sometimes they take the route of old soldiers.

Generic wines

A *generic name* is a wine name that has been used inappropriately for so long that the name has lost its original meaning in the eyes of the government (exactly what Xerox, Kleenex, and Band-Aid are afraid of becoming).

Burgundy, Chianti, Chablis, Champagne, Rhine wine, Sherry, Port, and Sauterne are all names that rightfully should apply only to wines made in those specific places. But these names have been usurped by very large and powerful wine companies. So now both the U.S. and Canadian governments recognize these names as broad *types* of wine rather than as wines from specific regions.

Most California wines carried generic names until the late '60s or early '70s when varietals came into vogue. Generics are still around, but they are less popular in the marketplace with every passing year.

When you buy a generic wine, you have absolutely no idea what you're getting except that the wine is a piece of history.

Chapter 5

Win(e)ding Up Satisfied: Picking Out Your Wines

In This Chapter

- Arming yourself against the forces of intimidation
- Selecting a good wine merchant
- Finding the help you need to get the wine you want
- Choosing the right wine
- Surviving the wine presentation ritual

Unless you enjoy a permanent, dependent relationship with an indulgent and knowledgeable wine lover, the day will come when you have to purchase a bottle of wine yourself. If you're lucky, the shop owner will just happen to be some enlightened fellow whose life purpose is to make good wine easy and accessible to others. If you're lucky, you'll also be awarded an honorary doctorate from Harvard and receive a tax-free inheritance from a great aunt you've never met. The odds are about equal.

When you buy a bottle of wine in a restaurant, you get to taste it right then and there: instant gratification. If you've chosen well, you have a delicious wine that pairs beautifully with the food you've selected. If you haven't chosen well . . . well, we all know *that* feeling!

In this chapter, we give you tips for navigating your way through a wine shop and a restaurant wine list, as well.

Experiencing the Wine Specialty Shop

Wine specialty shops are small- to medium-sized stores that sell wine and liquor and, sometimes, wine books, corkscrews (see Chapter 6 for more on those), wine glasses, and maybe a few specialty foods. The foods sold in wine shops tend to be gourmet items rather than just run-of-the-mill snack foods.

If you decide to pursue wine as a serious hobby, shops like these are the ones where you'll probably end up buying your wine because they offer many advantages that larger operations cannot. For one thing, wine specialty shops almost always have wine-knowledgeable staffers on the premises. Also, you can usually find an interesting, varied selection of wines at all price levels.

Wine shops often organize their wines by country of origin and — in the case of classic wine countries, such as France — by region (Bordeaux, Burgundy, Rhône, and so on). Red wines and white wines are often in separate sections within the country sections. They may have a special section for Champagnes and other sparkling wines and yet another section for dessert wines.

Over in a corner somewhere, usually right by the door to accommodate quick purchases, you often see a *cold box,* a refrigerated cabinet with glass doors where bottles of best-selling white and sparkling wines sit. Unless you really *must*

Four great things about buying wine in a store and drinking it at home

- Stores usually have a much bigger selection of wines than restaurants do.
- The wine is less expensive than in restaurants.
- You can touch the bottles and compare the labels.
- The guy who sells the wine to you can't watch you or listen to what you say when you're drinking it.

Ten clues for identifying a store where you should *not* buy wine

1. The dust on the wine bottles is more than ⅛-inch thick.
2. Most of the white wines are light brown in color.
3. The most recent vintage in the store is 1992.
4. The colors on all the wine labels have faded from bright sunlight.
5. The temperature inside the store is warmer than a sauna.
6. Most of the bottles are standing up.
7. All of the bottles are standing up!
8. The selection consists mainly of jug wines or "Bag-in-the-Box" wines.
9. The June Wine of the Month has a picture of Santa Claus on the label.
10. The owner resembles Darth Vader.

have an ice-cold bottle of wine immediately (you've decided to elope and the wedding toast is only ten minutes away), avoid the cold box. The wines are usually too cold and, therefore, may not be in good condition. You never know how long the bottle you select has been sitting in frigid conditions, numbed lifeless.

Choosing the Right Merchant

Sizing up a wine merchant is as simple as sizing up any other specialty retailer. The main criteria are fair prices, a wide selection, staff expertise, and service. Also, the shop must store its wines in the proper conditions. Here are some tips to keep in mind:

- **Put price in perspective:** When you're a novice wine buyer, your best strategy is to shop around with an eye to service and reliable advice more than to price. After you've found a merchant who has suggested several wines you've liked, stick with him, even if he doesn't have the best prices. Until you have the confidence to shop at stores with the better prices, it makes better sense to pay a dollar or so more for wines that are recommended by a reliable merchant.

- **Evaluate selection and expertise:** You won't necessarily know on your first visit whether a particular store's selection is adequate for you. If you notice many wines from many different countries at various prices, give the store's selection the benefit of the doubt. If you outgrow the selection as you learn more about wine, you can seek out a new merchant at that point.

Don't be too ready to give a merchant the benefit of the doubt when it comes to expertise. Some retailers are not only knowledgeable about the specific wines they sell, they're also knowledgeable about wine in general. Some retailers, however, know less than their customers. Ask questions (such as, "Can you tell me something about this wine?"), and judge how willing and able the merchant is to answer them. Expect a wine merchant to have *personal* knowledge and experience of the wines he sells and not just rely on the ratings of a few critics.

- **Expecting service with a smile:** Most knowledgeable wine merchants pride themselves in their ability to guide you through the maze of wine selections and help you find a wine that you will like. Trust a merchant's advice at least once or twice and see whether his choices are good ones. If he's not flexible enough — or knowledgeable enough — to suggest wine that suits your needs, obviously you need another merchant.

Any reputable wine merchant will accept a bottle back from you if he has made a poor recommendation or if the wine seems damaged. After all, he wants to keep you as a customer. But with the privilege comes responsibility: Be reasonable. You should return an *open* bottle only if you think the wine is defective (and then the bottle should be mostly full!). Hold on to the store's receipt. And don't wait several months before returning an unopened bottle of wine. After a week or two, consider the wine yours.

- **Judging wine storage conditions:** Here's a fact about wine that's worth learning early on: Wine is a perishable product. In sizing up a wine shop, check out the store's wine storage conditions. What you don't want to see is an area that's warm — for example, wines stored near the boiler so that they cook all winter. The very best shops will have climate-controlled storerooms for wine — although, frankly, these shops are in the minority.

In better wine shops, you'll see most of the bottles (except for the inexpensive, large, jug-like bottles) lying *in a horizontal position,* so that their corks remain moist, ensuring a firm closure. A dry cork can crack or shrink and let air into the bottle, which will spoil the wine.

Unfortunately, the problem of wine spoilage doesn't begin at the retail outlet. Quite frequently, the *wholesaler* or *distributor* — the company from which the retailer purchases wine — doesn't have proper storage conditions, either. A good retailer will check out the quality of the wine before he buys it, or he'll send the wine back if he discovers the problem after already buying the wine.

Strategies for Wine Shopping

When you get beyond all the ego-compromising innuendo associated with buying wine, you can really have fun in wine shops. We remember when we first caught the wine bug. We spent countless hours on Saturdays visiting different wine stores near our home. (To a passionate wine lover, 30 miles can be near.) Trips to other cities offered new opportunities to explore. So many wines, so little time. . . .

Naturally, we made our share of mistakes along the way, but we learned a lot of good lessons.

- **See a chance, take it:** When we first started buying wine, our repertoire was about as broad as a two-year-old child's vocabulary. We'd buy the same brands again and again because they were safe choices, we knew what to expect from them, and we liked them well enough — all good reasons to buy a particular wine. But we soon realized that if wine was really going to be fun, we had to be a little more adventuresome.
- **Explain what you want:** The following scene — or something very much like it — occurs in every wine shop every day (and ten times every Saturday):

  Customer: I remember that it's got a beige label. I had it in this little restaurant last week.

  Wine Merchant: Do you know what country it's from?

  Customer: No, but I think it has a flower on the label.

Four easy steps to getting a wine you like

Step One: Decide how much you want to spend on a bottle. Tell your wine merchant your price range; this will narrow the arena of wines to consider.

Step Two: Describe to your wine merchant the kind of wine you like in clear, simple terms. For white wine, you might use such words as "crisp, dry," or "fruity, ripe, oaky, buttery, full-bodied." For red wines, you might say "big, rich, tannic," or "medium-bodied, soft." (Turn to Chapter 2 to learn other helpful descriptors.)

Step Three: Tell your wine merchant what kind of food you plan to have with the wine, if you know. This will narrow down your choices even more.

Step Four: Ask for tasting samples, if they are available where you shop. (Stores often have wine samples available for tasting every Saturday, where legal.) Of course, the sample will probably come to you in a plastic cup and the temperature might not be ideal, but at least you'll get a general idea of whether or not it's your cup of tea.

Wine Merchant: Do you recall the vintage?

Customer: I think it's young, but I'm not sure. Maybe if I walk around, I can spot it.

Needless to say, most of the time that customer never finds the wine he or she is looking for.

When you come across a wine you like, write down as much specific information from the label as you can. Don't trust your memory. By the time you arrive in your wine store, you might not recall many details about the wine if you haven't written them down. If your wine merchant can see the name, he can give you that wine or — if he doesn't have that exact wine — he may be able to give you something very similar to it.

- **Name your price:** Because the price of a bottle of wine can range from $3 to — literally — hundreds of dollars, it's a good idea to decide approximately how much you want to spend and to tell your wine merchant. A good retailer with an adequate selection should be able to make several wine suggestions in your preferred price category.

The Restaurant Wine Experience

Here and there, you might come across a restaurant with a retail wine shop on the premises, a useful hybrid of a place where you can look over all the bottles, read the labels, browse through wine books and magazines, and then carry your chosen bottle to your table. Unfortunately, such establishments are rarer than four-leaf clovers. In most restaurants, you have to choose your wine from a menu that tells you only the names of the wines and the price per bottle. Welcome to the *restaurant wine list.*

Restaurant wine lists can be infuriating: All too frequently, the lists simply are not accurate, and you spend ten good minutes of your life deciding which wine to order, only to discover that it's "not available tonight" (and probably hasn't been for months). But don't give up without a fight. With a little guidance and a few tips, you can navigate the choppy waters of the wine list.

How Wine Is Sold in Restaurants

Believe it or not, restaurateurs really do want you to buy their wine. They usually make a sizable profit on every sale, their servers earn bigger tips and become happier employees, and you enjoy your meal more, going home a happier customer.

Wines available for sale in a restaurant these days generally fall into four categories: house wines, premium wines, wines available by the bottle from the restaurant's regular wine list, and rarer wines available from a special wine list, sometimes called a *reserve wine list.* Not all restaurants offer all four categories.

- The *house wines,* usually one white and one red, and sometimes also a sparkling wine. These can be purchased *by the glass* or in a *carafe* (a wide-mouthed handle-less pitcher). They are the wines you get when you simply ask for a glass of white or a glass of red.
- *Premium* wines, available by the glass. These offer a wider selection than the house wines and are generally better quality. (These wines are usually available also by the bottle.)

The choice of the house

The restaurant's *house wines* are often some inferior stuff that the restaurant owner is making an enormous profit on. House wines can range in price from $3 up to $8 a glass (with an average of $5 to $6). Often, the entire bottle costs the proprietor the price of one glass, or less! No wonder the "obliging" server fills your glass to the brim.

If the house wine is your only option, ask the server what it is. Don't be satisfied with the response, "It's Chardonnay"; ask for specifics. Chardonnay from where? What brand? Ask to see the bottle. Either your worst fears will be confirmed (you've never heard of the wine, or it has a reputation for being inferior), or you'll be pleasantly surprised (you *have* heard of the wine, and it has a good reputation). At least you'll know what you're drinking, for future reference.

Premium pours

The word *premium* is used very loosely by the wine industry. When annual industry sales statistics are compiled for the U.S., *premium* indicates any wine that sells for more than $7 a bottle in stores. As used in the phrase *premium wines by the glass,* however, *premium* usually does connote better quality. These are red and white wines that a restaurant offers at a higher price than its basic house wines. Premium wines are usually in the $6 to $12 price range per glass.

These premium wines are not anonymous beverages, like the house red and white, but are identified for you on the wine list, on a separate card, verbally, or sometimes even by a display of bottles. Ordering premium wines by the glass is a fine idea, especially if you want to have only a glass or two or if you and your guests want to experiment by trying several wines. Sometimes we order a glass of a premium white wine or a glass of Champagne as a starter and then go on to a bottle of red wine.

Of course, there's a catch. Only a small percentage of restaurants — the "wine-conscious" ones — offer premium wines by the glass. Also, you'll end up paying more for the wine if you order a bottle's worth of individual glasses than you would if you ordered a whole bottle to begin with.

Special, or reserve, wine lists

Some restaurants — only a few, and usually the fanciest — offer a special wine list of rare wines to supplement their regular wine list. These special lists appeal to two types of customers: very serious wine connoisseurs and "high rollers." If you're not in either category, don't even bother asking if the restaurant has such a list. Then again, if you're not paying for the meal or if you seriously want to impress a client or a date, you might want to look at it! Try to get help with the special list from some knowledgeable person on the restaurant staff, though: Any mistake you make could be a costly one.

The (anything but) standard wine list

Most of the time, you'll probably end up turning to the restaurant's standard wine list to choose your wine. We use the term *standard wine list* to distinguish a restaurant's basic wine list from its special, or reserve, wine list. Unfortunately, there's nothing standard about wine lists at all. Which is why the next section in this book covers . . .

How to Scope Out a Wine List

Your first step in the dark encounter between you and the wine list is to size up the opposition. You can do this by noting how the wine list is organized.

Read the headings on the wine list the way you'd read the chapter titles in a book you were considering buying. Figure out how the wines are categorized and how they're arranged within each category. Notice how much or how little information is given about each wine. Check out the style of the list: Does it seem pretentious or straightforward? Estimate the number of wines on the list — 12 or 200.

Sizing up the organization of the list

Predicting exactly what you'll find on the list, other than prices, is impossible. Generally speaking, though, you may discover the wines arranged in the following categories:

- Champagne and sparkling wines
- (Dry) white wines
- (Dry) red wines
- Dessert wines

Some restaurants further subdivide the wines on their list according to country, especially in the white and red wine categories: French red wines, Italian red wines, American reds, and so on. These country sections might then be subdivided by wine region. France, for example, might have listings of Bordeaux, Burgundy, and possibly Rhône all under *French red wines. USA reds* may be divided into California wines, Oregon wines, and Washington wines.

Or you might find that the categories under white wines and red wines are the names of grape varieties — for example, a Chardonnay section, a Sauvignon Blanc section, and a miscellaneous *other dry whites* section, all under the general heading of white wines. If the restaurant features a particular country's cuisine, the wines of that country might be listed first (and given certain prominence), followed by a cursory listing of wines from other areas.

Often you'll find that within each category, the wines are arranged in ascending order of price with the least expensive wine first. Many a restaurateur is betting that you won't order that first wine out of fear of looking cheap. They figure you'll go for the second, third, or fourth wine down the price column or even deeper if you're feeling insecure and need the reassurance that your choice is a good one. (Meanwhile, that least expensive wine might be perfectly fine.)

What the wine list should tell you

The more serious a restaurant is about its wine selection, the more information it gives you about each wine. Here's some information that's likely to be on the wine list:

- An *item number* for each wine. These are sometimes called *bin numbers,* referring to the specific location of each wine in the restaurant's cellar or wine storage room. Item numbers make it easier for the server to locate and pull the wine quickly. They're also a crutch for *you* in ordering the wine in case you don't have a clue how to pronounce what you've decided to drink.
- The name of each wine. These names might be grape names or place-names (refer to Chapter 4), but they had better also include the name of each producer (Château this, or that Winery), or you'll have no way of knowing exactly which wine any listing is meant to represent.
- A vintage indication for each wine — the year that the grapes were harvested. If the wine is a blend of wines from different years, it might say *NV,* for *non-vintage.* Sometimes, you'll see *VV,* which means that the wine is a vintage-dated wine, but you're not allowed to know *which* vintage it is unless you ask. The restaurateur just doesn't want to bother changing the year on the list when the wine's vintage changes.
- Sometimes, suggestions from the restaurateur for certain wines to go with their dinner entrées. In our experience, this information is helpful at times, but you might not always like — or agree with — their wine suggestion.
- Prices. You will *always* see a price for each wine.

Assessing the list's style

Once upon a time, the best wine lists consisted of hand-lettered pages inside heavy leather covers embossed with the words *Carte des Vins* in gold. Today, the best wine lists are more likely to be laser-printed pages or cards that more than make up in functionality what they sacrifice in romance.

The world's most complicated wine list

We've heard that there's a restaurant in Colorado whose wine list is like this:

"1. White wine

2. Red wine

3. Rosé wine

To avoid confusing the waiter, please order your wine by number."

The more permanent and immutable a wine list seems, the less accurate its listings are likely to be — and the less specific. Such lists suggest that no one is really looking after wine on a day-to-day basis in that restaurant. Chances are that many of the wines listed will be out of stock.

How to Ask for Advice

If, after sizing up the wine list, you decide that you are not familiar with most of the wines on it, ask for help with your selection.

If the restaurant is a fancy one, ask if there's a *sommelier* (pronounced *som-mel-yay*) — technically, a specially trained, high-level wine specialist who is responsible for putting the wine list together and for making sure that the wines offered on the list complement the cuisine of the restaurant. (Unfortunately, only a few restaurants employ one — usually the most wine-conscious.)

If the restaurant is not particularly fancy, ask to speak with the wine specialist. Often someone on the staff, frequently the proprietor, knows the wine list well.

If someone on the restaurant staff knows the wine list well, he or she will usually know what wines go best with the food you are ordering. He will also be extremely appreciative of your interest in the list. For these reasons, even though we are familiar with wine, we often consult the sommelier, proprietor, or wine specialist for wine list suggestions.

Here are some face-saving methods of getting help:

- If you're not sure how to pronounce the wine's name, point to it on the list, or use the wine's item or bin number (if there is one).
- Point out two or three wines on the list to the sommelier or server and say, "I'm considering these wines. Which one do you recommend?" This is also a subtle way of communicating your price range.
- Ask to *see* one or two bottles; the labels might help you make up your mind.
- Ask if there are any half-bottles (375 ml) or 500 ml bottles available (sometimes they're not listed). Smaller bottles give you wider possibilities in ordering: For example, you might drink a half bottle of white wine and a half or full (750 ml) bottle of red wine.
- Mention the food you plan to order and ask for suggestions of wines that would complement the meal.

How to Ace the Wine Presentation Ritual

In many restaurants, the wine presentation occurs with such solemnity and ceremony that you'd think you were involved in high church or temple services. The hushed tones of the waiter, the ritualized performance — the seriousness of it all can make you want to laugh (but that seems wrong — like laughing in church). At the very least, you might be tempted to tell your waiter, "Lighten up! It's just a bottle of fermented fruit juice!"

Actually, though, there's some logic behind the Wine Presentation Ritual. Step by step, the Ritual (and the logic) goes like this:

1. **The waiter or sommelier presents the bottle to you (assuming that you are the person who ordered the wine) for inspection.** The point of this procedure is to make sure that the bottle *is* the bottle you ordered. If you're satisfied with the bottle, nod your approval.

2. **The server then removes the cork and places it in front of you.** The purpose of this step is for you to determine, by smelling and visually inspecting the cork, whether the cork is in good condition, and whether the cork seems to be the legitimate cork for that bottle of wine. If the cork does raise your suspicions, you should still wait to smell or taste the wine itself before rejecting the bottle.
3. **If your wine needs decanting, the server will decant it at this point.** For more information on decanting, see Chapter 6.
4. **The server pours a small amount of wine into your glass and waits.** At this point, you're *not* supposed to say, "Is that all you're giving me?!" You're expected to take a sniff of the wine, perhaps a little sip, and then either nod your approval to the waiter or murmur, "It's fine." Actually, this is an important step of the Wine Presentation Ritual because if something is *wrong* with the wine, *now* is the time to return it (not after you've finished half of the bottle!). For a review of wine-tasting technique, turn to Chapter 2 before you head out to the restaurant.

If you're not really sure whether the condition of the wine is acceptable, ask for someone else's opinion at your table and then make a group decision; otherwise, you risk feeling foolish by either returning the bottle later when it's been declared defective by one of your guests, or by drinking the stuff when it becomes clear to you later that there's something wrong with it.

If you do decide that the bottle is out of condition, describe to the server what you find wrong with the wine, using the best language you can. (*Musty* or *dank* are descriptors that are easily understood.) Let him smell or taste the wine himself if he would like. But don't let him make you feel guilty.

Depending on whether the sommelier or captain agrees that it's a bad bottle or whether he believes that you just don't understand the wine, he might bring you another bottle of the same, or he might bring you the wine list so that you can select a different wine. Either way, the Ritual begins again from the top.

Twice the price

A few profit-minded restaurateurs train their servers to maximize wine sales in every way possible — even at the customers' expense. For example, some servers are trained to refill wine glasses liberally so that the bottle is emptied before the main course arrives. (This can happen all the more easily when the glasses are large.) Upon emptying the bottle, the server asks, "Shall I bring another bottle of the same wine?" Depending on how much wine is in everyone's glass and how much wine your guests tend to drink, you might not *need* another bottle, but your tendency will be to say yes to avoid looking stingy.

An even trickier practice is to refill the glasses starting with the host, so that the bottle runs dry before each of the guests has had a refill. How can you refuse a second bottle at the expense of your guests' enjoyment?! You'll have to order that second bottle — and you should let the manager know how you feel about it when you leave. (But remember, these nefarious restaurant practices are the exception rather than the rule.)

5. **If you do accept the wine, the waiter will pour the wine into your guests' glasses and then finally into yours. Now you're allowed to relax.**

Restaurant Wining Tips

Wining in restaurants requires so many decisions that you really do need a guidebook. Should you leave the wine in an ice bucket? What should you do if the wine is bad? And can you bring your own wine? Let the following tips guide you:

- **Can I kick the ice-bucket habit?** Most servers assume that an ice bucket is necessary to chill white wines and sparkling wines. But sometimes the bottle is already so cold when it comes to you that the wine would be better off warming up a bit on the table. If your white wine goes into an ice bucket and you think it's getting *too* cold, remove it from the bucket, or have the waiter remove it.

Sometimes, a red wine that's a bit too warm can benefit from five or ten minutes in an ice bucket. (But be careful! It can get too cold very quickly.) If the server acts as if you're nuts to chill a red wine, ignore him.

- **What's with these tiny glasses?** When various glasses are available, you can exercise your right to choose a different glass from the one you were given. If the restaurant's red wine glass is quite small, a stemmed water glass might be more appropriate for the red wine.
- **Should the wine "breathe"?** If a red wine you ordered needs aeration to soften its harsh tannins (see Chapter 6), merely pulling the cork will be practically useless in accomplishing that (because the air space at the neck of the bottle is too small). Decanting the bottle or pouring the wine into glasses is the best tactic.
- **Where's my bottle?** We prefer to have our bottle of wine on or near our table, not out of our reach. We can look at the label that way, and we don't have to wait for the server to remember to refill our glasses, either.
- **What if the bottle is bad?** Refuse any bottle that tastes or smells unpleasant (unless you brought it yourself!). A good restaurateur will always replace the wine, even if he thinks there's nothing wrong with it.
- **May I bring my own wine?** Some restaurants allow you to bring your own wine — especially if you express the desire to bring a special wine, or an older wine. Restaurants will usually charge a *corkage* fee (a fee for wine service, use of the glasses, and so on) that can vary from $10 to even $25 a bottle, depending on the attitude of the restaurant. You should never bring a wine that is already on the restaurant's wine list; it's cheap and it's insulting. You should call ahead to determine whether it's possible to bring wine (in some places, the restaurant's license prohibits it) and to ask what the corkage fee is.
- **What if I'm traveling abroad?** If you journey to countries where wine is made, such as France, Italy, Germany, Switzerland, Austria, Spain, or Portugal, by all means try the local wines. They will be fresher than the imports, in good condition, and the best values on the wine list.

Chapter 6

Everything You Need to Know about Serving and Using Wine

In This Chapter

- Corkophobia and other barriers to getting the wine out
- Breathing lessons for your bottle
- Tulips, flutes, trumpets, and other types of wine glasses
- Survival tactics for leftover wine

Have you ever broken a cork while trying to extract it from the bottle, or taken an unusually long time to remove a stubborn cork while your guests smiled at you uneasily? This has certainly happened to each of us from time to time and probably to just about everyone else who has ever pulled a cork out of a bottle of wine. It's enough to give anyone a case of corkophobia!

Removing the cork from a wine bottle is the first challenge that faces you in your quest to enjoy wine, and it's a big one. (Fortunately, once you get the hang of doing so, the cork removal is easy — most of the time.) Afterwards, you're faced with the niggling details of wine service, such as which type of glass to use and what to do if you don't finish the whole bottle. But help is now at hand for those who are wine-challenged!

Getting the Cork Out

Before you can even think about removing the cork from a wine bottle, you need to deal with whatever covers the cork.

Most wine bottles have a colorful covering over the cork end of the bottle that's called a *capsule*. These days, most wineries use colored foil or plastic capsules rather than the traditional lead capsules. Some wineries use a transparent cellophane covering that lets the cork show through; often, the sheer look graces special *flange-top* bottles, a fancy wine bottle with a protruding, flat lip at the top. (Some flange-top bottles sport colorful plastic plugs on top of the cork instead.)

Whether the capsule is plastic, foil, or cellophane, we usually remove the entire capsule, so that no wine can possibly come into contact with the covering when we pour. (We use the small knife that's part of most *corkscrews* — the devices that exist solely for opening wine bottles.) When we encounter a plastic plug atop the cork instead of a capsule, we just flick it off with the tip of a knife.

After removing the capsule or plug, we wipe clean the top of the bottle with a damp cloth. Sometimes the visible end of the cork is dark with mold that developed under the capsule, and in that case, we wipe the top all the more diligently. (If you encounter mold atop the cork, don't be concerned. That mold is actually a good sign: It means that the wine has been stored in humid conditions.)

Traditional wine etiquette dictates that you do not remove the entire capsule. Therefore, many people use a gizmo called a foil cutter that sells for about $6 or $7 in wine shops, kitchen stores, or specialty catalogs. However, the foil cutter does not cut the capsule low enough, in our opinion, to prevent wine from dripping over the edge of the foil into your glass. If you want to leave the capsule on, be sure to cut the foil with a knife under the second lip of the bottle.

The right tools

Corkophobia or not, anyone can conquer most corks with a good corkscrew. Struggling over a puny piece of cork with a second-rate corkscrew will surely put you in a miserable mood before you even pour a drop.

The corkscrew not to use

The one corkscrew we absolutely avoid happens to be the most common type of corkscrew around. We're talking about the infamous Wing Type Corkscrew, a bright silver-colored, metal device that looks something like a pair of pliers; when you insert this corkscrew into a cork, two "wings" open out from the side of the corkscrew. We don't like it for one very simple reason: It mangles the cork, almost guaranteeing that brown flakes will be floating in your glass of wine.

Invest a few dollars in a decent corkscrew. The time and hassle you save will be more than worth the investment. Of the many types of wine-bottle openers available, we recommend the three described in the following sections.

The corkscrew to buy

The one indispensable corkscrew for every household is the Screwpull. The Screwpull is about six inches long. It's made of plastic and has a 5-inch worm that's coated with Teflon (see Figure 6-1). To use this corkscrew, you simply place the plastic over the bottle top (having removed the capsule) until a lip on the plastic is resting on the top of the bottle. Insert the worm through the plastic until it touches the cork. Hold on to the plastic firmly while turning the lever atop the worm clockwise. The worm descends into the cork. Simply keep turning the lever in the same clockwise direction, and the cork magically emerges from the bottle. To remove the cork from the Screwpull, simply turn the lever counterclockwise while holding on to the cork.

The Screwpull comes in many colors — burgundy, black, and China red being the most common — and costs in the $20 range in wine shops, kitchen stores, and specialty catalogs. The Screwpull is very simple to use, doesn't require a lot of muscle, and is our corkscrew of choice for *most* of the corks that we encounter.

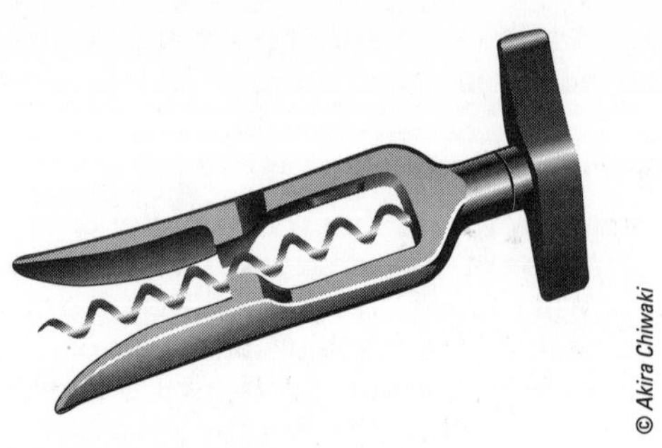

© Akira Chiwaki

Figure 6-1: The Screwpull corkscrew.

Other corkscrews worth owning

Did we say most? Well, you see, that's why we have two other corkscrews for the remaining corks that the Screwpull can't remove (or threatens to break itself on; after all, the Screwpull is mostly plastic, and $20 is $20). Flange-top bottles, for example, really challenge the Screwpull because of their unusual width at the top.

The two-pronged type used in California

One of the corkscrews is called, unofficially, the Ah-So because (according to wine legend, anyway) when people finally figure out how it works, they say, "Ah, so that's how it works!"

The Ah-So is a simple device made up of two thin, flat metal prongs, one slightly longer than the other (see Figure 6-2). To use this corkscrew, you slide the prongs down into the tight space between the cork and the bottle (inserting the longer prong first), using a back-and-forth seesaw motion until the top of the Ah-So is resting on the top of the cork, then twist the cork while gently pulling up. You end up with an intact cork that you can reuse. The Ah-So sells for around $6 to $8.

Although more difficult to operate than the Screwpull, the Ah-So really handles very tight-fitting corks that no other corkscrews, including the Screwpull, seem to be able to budge. Also, the Ah-So can be effective with old, crumbly corks in which other corkscrews cannot get a proper grip — although the Ah-So is useless with loose corks that move around in the bottle's neck when you try to remove them. The corkscrew just pushes those corks down into the wine. At that point, you'll need another tool called a *cork retriever* (which we describe in the "Waiter, there's cork in my wine!" section, later in this chapter).

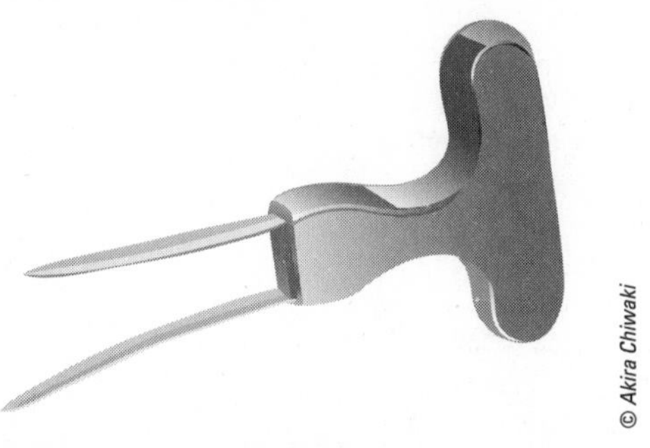

Figure 6-2: The Ah-So corkscrew.

The most professional corkscrew of them all

Our final recommended corkscrew, probably the most commonly used corkscrew in restaurants all over the world, is simply called the Waiter's Corkscrew. A straight metal base holds three devices that fold into it, like a Swiss Army knife: a lever; a small, two-inch worm; and a little knife (see Figure 6-3) that's especially handy for removing the capsule from the bottle. The Waiter's Corkscrew sells for as little as $7, but designer versions can cost more than ten times that much.

Figure 6-3: The Waiter's Corkscrew.

Using the Waiter's Corkscrew requires some practice. First, wrap a fist around the bottle's neck. The trick then is to guide the worm down through the center of the cork by turning the

The comeback of the screwcap

Instead of cork or imitation cork, we'd prefer to see real screwcaps on most wine bottles. Screwcaps are perfectly sound closures, technically speaking. And they prevent "cork taint," a chemical flaw affecting a small percentage of corks, and consequently the wine inside those bottles. A "corky" wine — that is, one affected with cork taint — is damaged either slightly or flagrantly. In the worst-case scenarios, corky wines give off an offensive odor similar to moldy or damp cardboard.

Formerly, only the least expensive, lower-quality wines had screwcap closures. But recently, as a reaction to the corky wine problem, more and more wine producers have been switching from corks to screwcaps. Is this the start of a movement? Fine with us.

corkscrew; turn slowly at first, until you're sure that the worm is descending down the middle of the cork rather than the side. After the worm is fully descended into the cork, place the lever on the lip of the bottle and push against the lever while lifting up the cork. Give a firm pull at the very end or wiggle out the bottom of the cork with your hand.

If your cork ever breaks and part of it gets stuck in the neck of the bottle, the Waiter's Corkscrew is indispensable for removing the remaining piece. Use the method we just described, but insert the worm at a 45-degree angle instead. In most cases, you will successfully remove the broken cork.

Waiter, there's cork in my wine!

Every now and then, even if you've used the right corkscrew and used it properly, you can still have pieces of cork floating in your wine — even the entire cork.

Before you start berating yourself for being a klutz, know that "floating cork" has happened to all of us at one time or another, no matter how experienced we are. Cork won't harm the wine. And besides, a wonderful instrument called a *cork retriever* (no, it's not a small dog from the south of Ireland!) is available in specialty stores and in catalogs. The cork retriever consists of three 10-inch pieces of stiff metal wire with hooks on the ends.

This device is remarkably effective in removing floating pieces of cork from the bottle.

Alternatively, you can just pick out the offending piece(s) of cork with a spoon after you pour the wine into your glass. (That's one occasion when you'd be rude to serve your guest first, because the first glass has more cork pieces in it.) Or you can pour the wine through a paper coffee filter (preferably rinsed with hot water, to remove the chemicals) into a decanter to catch the remaining pieces of cork.

Opening Champagne and Sparkling Wine

Opening a bottle of sparkling wine is often an exciting occasion. Who doesn't enjoy the ceremony of a cold glass of bubbly? But you need to use a completely different technique than you'd use to open a regular wine bottle. The cork even looks different. Sparkling wine corks have a mushroom-shaped head that protrudes from the bottle and a wire cage that holds the cork in place against the pressure that's trapped inside the bottle.

Never, ever use a corkscrew on a bottle of sparkling wine. The pressure of the trapped carbonation, when suddenly released, could send the cork *and* corkscrew flying right into your eye.

Forget how the victors do it in locker rooms

If your bottle of bubbly has just traveled, let it rest for a while, preferably a day. Controlling the cork is difficult when the carbonation has been stirred up. (Hey, you wouldn't open a large bottle of warm soda that's been shaken up, either, would you? Sparkling wine has much more carbonated pressure than soda and needs more time to settle down.)

If you're in the midst of a sparkling wine emergency and need to open the bottle anyway, one quick solution is to calm down the carbonation by submerging the bottle in an ice bucket for about 30 minutes. (Fill the bucket with one-half ice cubes and one-half ice-cold water.)

In any case, be careful when you remove the wire cage and keep one hand on top of the cork as a precaution. Be sure to point the bottle away from people and other fragile objects.

A sigh is better than a pop

If you like to hear the sparkling wine pop, just yank the cork out. When you do that, however, you'll lose some of the precious wine, which will froth out of the bottle. Also, the noise could interfere with your guests' conversation. Besides, it ain't too classy!

Removing the cork from sparkling wine with just a gentle sigh rather than a loud pop is fairly easy. Simply hold the bottle at a 45-degree angle with a towel wrapped around the bottle if it's wet. (Try resting the base of the bottle on your hipbone.) Twist the bottle while holding on to the cork so that you can control the cork as it emerges. When you feel the cork starting to come out of the bottle, *push down against the cork* with some pressure as if you don't want to let it out of the bottle. In this way, the cork will emerge slowly with a hissing or sighing sound rather than a pop.

Every once in a while, you'll come across a really tight cork that doesn't want to budge. Try running the top of the bottle under warm water for a few moments, or wrapping a towel around it to create friction. Either one of these actions will usually enable you to remove the cork.

Another option is to purchase a fancy gadget resembling a pair of pliers (there are actually three gadgets: Champagne Pliers, a Champagne Star, and a Champagne Key) that you place around the part of the cork that's outside the bottle. Or you could probably try using regular pliers, although lugging in the toolbox will surely change the mood of the occasion.

Does Wine Really Breathe?

Most wine is alive in the sense that the wine changes chemically as it slowly grows older. Wine absorbs oxygen and, like our own cells, oxidizes. When the grapes turn into wine in the first place, they give off carbon dioxide, just like us. So we suppose you can say that wine breathes, in a sense.

That's not what the server means when he asks, "Shall I pull the cork and let the wine breathe, sir (or madam)?" The term *breathing* usually refers to the process of aerating the wine, which means exposing the wine to air. But just pulling the cork out of the bottle and letting the bottle sit there is a truly ineffective way to aerate the wine. The little space at the neck of the bottle is way too small to allow your wine to breathe.

How to aerate your wine

If you really want to aerate your wine, do one or both of the following:

1. Pour the wine into a *decanter* (a fancy word for a glass container that is big enough to hold the contents of an entire bottle of wine).
2. Pour the wine into large glasses at least ten minutes before you plan to drink it.

Practically speaking, what your decanter looks like or how much it costs doesn't matter. In fact, the very inexpensive, wide-mouthed carafes are fine.

Which wines need aerating?

Many red wines but only a few white wines — and some dessert wines — can benefit from aeration. You can drink most white wines upon pouring, unless they're too cold, but that's a discussion for later.

Young, tannic red wines

Young red wines, especially those that are high in tannin (refer to Chapter 2 for more on tannin) — such as Cabernet Sauvignons, Bordeaux, many wines from the Rhône Valley, and many Italian wines — actually taste better with aeration because their tannins soften and the wine becomes less harsh.

The younger and more tannic the wine is, the longer it needs to breathe. As a general rule, however, most tannic, young red wines soften up with one hour of aeration.

Older red wines with sediment

Many red wines develop *sediment* (tannin and other matter in the wine that solidifies over time) usually after about eight years of age. The sediment can taste a bit bitter (remember, it's tannin). Also, the dark particles floating in your wine, usually near the bottom of your glass, don't look very appetizing.

To remove sediment, keep the bottle of wine upright at least a day or two before you plan to open it so that the sediment settles at the bottom of the bottle. Then decant the wine carefully: Pour the wine out of the bottle slowly into a decanter while watching the wine inside the bottle as it approaches the neck. Stop pouring when you see cloudy wine from the bottom of the bottle making its way to the neck. When you stop pouring at the right moment, all the cloudy wine remains behind in the bottle.

The older the wine, the more delicate the wine can be. Don't give old, fragile-looking wines excessive aeration. (Look at the color of the wine through the bottle before you decant; if the color looks pale, the wine could be pretty far along its maturity curve.) The flavors of really old wines will start fading rapidly after 10 or 15 minutes of air exposure. However, if the wine has a dark color, chances are that the wine is still quite youthful and will need to breathe more.

A few white wines

Some very good, dry white wines — such as full-bodied white Burgundies and white Bordeaux wines, as well as the best Alsace whites — also get better with aeration. For example, if you open up a young Corton-Charlemagne (a great white Burgundy), and it doesn't seem to be showing much aroma or flavor, chances are that the wine needs aeration. Decant the wine and try it again in half an hour. In most cases, your wine will dramatically improve.

Vintage Ports

One of the most famous fortified wines is Vintage Port (properly called "Porto"), which is usually not *mature* (ready to drink) until about 20 years after the vintage.

For now, we'll just say that, yes, Vintage Port needs breathing lessons, very much so indeed! Young Vintage Ports are so brutally tannic that they demand many hours of aeration (eight would not be too much). Even older Ports will improve with four hours or more of aeration. Older Vintage Ports require decanting for another reason: They are chock-full of sediment. Keep Vintage Ports standing for several days before you open them.

Exceptions to the "decant your red wines and Ports" rule

The exceptions prove the rule. The majority of red wines you drink do not require decanting, aeration, or any special preparation other than pulling the cork out and having a glass handy. The following red wines *do not* need decanting:

- Lighter-bodied, less tannic red wines, such as Pinot Noir, Burgundy, Beaujolais, and Côtes du Rhône; lighter red Zinfandels; and lighter-bodied Italian reds, such as Dolcetto, Barberas, and lighter Chianti. These wines don't have much tannin and don't need much aeration.
- Inexpensive (less than $12) red wines. Same reason as preceding.
- Tawny ports — in fact, any other Ports except Vintage Ports. These wines should be free from sediment (which stayed behind in the barrels where the wine aged) and are ready to drink when you pour them.

Does the Glass Really Matter?

If you're just drinking wine as refreshment with your meal, and you aren't thinking about the wine much as it goes down, the glass you use probably doesn't matter in the least. A jelly glass? Why not? Plastic glasses? We've used them dozens of times on picnics, not to mention in airplanes (where the wine's quality usually doesn't demand great glasses, anyway).

If you have a good wine, a special occasion, friends who want to talk about the wine with you, or the boss for dinner, *stemware* (glasses with stems) is called for. And it's not just a question of etiquette and status: Good wine tastes better out of good glasses. Really.

The right color: none

Good wine glasses are always clear. Those pink or green glasses may look nice in your china cabinet, but they interfere with your ability to distinguish the true colors of the wine.

Thin but not tiny

Believe it or not, the taste of a wine changes when you drink the wine out of different types of glasses. Three aspects of a glass are important: the size, the shape, and the thickness of the glass.

- **Size:** For dry red and white wine, small glasses are anathema. You just can't swirl the wine around in those little glasses without spilling it, which makes appreciating the aroma of the wine almost impossible. Small glasses can work adequately only for sherry or dessert wines, which have strong aromas to begin with and are generally consumed in smaller quantities than table wines. But in most cases, larger is usually better.

  - Glasses for red wines should hold a minimum of 12 ounces; many of the best glasses have capacities ranging from 16 to 24 ounces, or more.
  - For white wines, 10 to 12 ounces minimum capacity.
  - For sparkling wines, 8 to 12 ounces is fine.

- **Thickness and shape:** Stemware made of very thin, fine crystal costs a lot more than normal glasses. That's one reason why many people don't use it, and why some people do. The better reason for using fine crystal is that the wine tastes better out of it.

  The shape of the bowl also matters. Some wine glasses have very round bowls, whereas others have more elongated, somewhat narrower bowls. We discuss the functions of various glass shapes in the next section.

Tulips, flutes, trumpets, and other picturesque wine-glass names

You thought that a tulip was a flower and a flute was a musical instrument? Well, they also happen to be types of glasses designed for use with sparkling wine. The tulip is the ideally shaped glass for bubblies (see Figure 6-4) — tall, elongated, and narrower at the rim than in the middle of the bowl. This shape helps hold the bubbles in the wine longer, not allowing them to escape freely.

The flute is another good sparkling wine glass (see Figure 6-5); but the flute is less ideal than the tulip because the flute does not narrow at the mouth. The trumpet actually widens at the mouth, making the glass less suitable for sparkling wine but very elegant looking (see Figure 6-6). Another drawback of the trumpet glass is that, depending on the design, the wine could actually fill the whole stem, which means the wine warms up from the heat of your hand as you hold the stem. Avoid the trumpet glass, which has no useful purpose as a wine glass.

Figure 6-4: The tulip glass for sparkling wine.

Figure 6-5: The flute glass for sparkling wine.

Figure 6-6: The trumpet glass for sparkling wine.

An oval-shaped bowl that is narrow at its mouth (see Figure 6-7) is ideal for many red wines, such as Bordeaux, Cabernet Sauvignon, Merlot, Chianti, and Zinfandel. On the other hand, some red wines, such as Burgundy, Pinot Noir, and Barolo, are best appreciated in wider-bowled, apple-shaped glasses. Which shape and size works best for which wine has to do with issues such as how the glass's shape controls the flow of wine onto your tongue.

To leave some margin of safety for swirling and smelling the wine, fill the wine glass only partially. One-third capacity, at the most, is the best fill-level for serious red wines. (This goes back to that idea of aerating the wine.) White wine glasses can be filled halfway, while sparkling wines can be three-quarters full.

Figure 6-7: The Bordeaux glass.

How many glasses do I need, anyway?

So what's a wine lover to do: Buy different glasses for each kind of wine? Fortunately, some all-purpose red and white wine glasses combine the best features, in terms of size, thickness, and shape, of most glasses. And you don't have to pay a fortune for decent glassware.

Washing your wine glasses

Detergents often leave a filmy residue in glasses, which can affect the aroma and flavor of your wine. We strongly advise that you clean your good crystal glasses by hand, using washing soda or baking soda. (Washing soda is the better of the two; it doesn't cake up, like baking soda.) Neither product leaves any soapy, filmy residue in your glass. You can find washing soda in the soap/detergent section of supermarkets.

Serving Wine Not Too Warm, Not Too Cold

Just as the right glass will enhance your wine experience, serving wine at the ideal temperature is a vital factor in your enjoyment of wine. Frequently, we've tasted the same wine at different temperatures (and, believe it or not, at different barometric pressures) and have loved the wine on one occasion but disliked it on the other!

Most red wines are at their best at cool room temperature, 62° to 65°F (16° to 18°C). Today when you hear room temperature, you think of a room that's about 70°F (21°C), don't you? Red wine served at this temperature can taste flat, flabby, lifeless, and often too *hot* — you get a burning sensation from the alcohol.

Ten or fifteen minutes in the fridge will do wonders to revive red wines that have been suffering from heat prostration, but red wines served too cold taste overly tannic and acidic, decidedly unpleasant. Light, fruity red wines, such as Beaujolais, are most delightful when served slightly chilled at about 58° to 60°F (14° to 15.5°C).

Are you wondering how to know when your bottle is 58° to 60°F? Although nifty thermometers are made just for that purpose, we have the two most common types, and we never use them. Just feel the bottle with your hand and take a guess. Practice makes perfect.

Just as many red wines are served too warm, most white wines are definitely served too cold. The higher the quality of a white wine, the less cold it should be so that you can properly appreciate its flavor.

To avoid the problem of warm bubbly, keep an ice bucket handy. Or put the bottle back in the refrigerator between pourings.

Storing Leftover Wine

A sparkling-wine stopper, a device that fits over an opened bottle, is really effective in keeping any remaining Champagne or sparkling wine fresh (often for several days) in the refrigerator. But what do you do when you have red or white wine left in the bottle?

You can put the cork back in the bottle if it still fits, and put the bottle into the refrigerator. (Even red wines will stay fresher there; just take the bottle out to warm up a couple of hours before serving it.) Or try these other methods:

- If you have about half a bottle of wine left, you can simply pour the wine into a clean, empty half-sized wine bottle and recork the smaller bottle.
- In most wine stores, you can buy a handy, inexpensive, miniature pump called a Vac-U-Vin. This pump removes the oxygen from the bottle, and the rubber stoppers that come with it prevent additional oxygen from entering the bottle.
- You can buy small cans of inert gas in some wine stores. Just squirt a few shots of the gas into the bottle through a skinny straw, which comes with the can, and put the cork back in the bottle. The gas displaces the oxygen in the bottle, thus protecting the wine from oxidizing.
- A new device, called WineSavor, is a flexible plastic disk that you roll up and insert down the bottle's neck. Once inside the bottle, the disk opens up and floats on top of the wine, blocking the wine from oxygen.

To avoid all this bother, just drink the wine! Or, if you're not too fussy, just place the leftover wine in the refrigerator and drink it in the next day or two.

Entertaining with Wine

When you're hosting a dinner party, you'll probably serve more wines than you would in the course of a normal dinner. Instead of just one wine all through the meal, you might want to serve a different wine with every course. Many people serve two wines at the table: a white with the first course and a red with the entrée. (And if they love wine, they'll use a cheese course as an excuse to serve a second, knockout red.)

Because you want every wine to taste even better than the one before it — besides blending perfectly with the food you serve — give some thought to the sequence in which you serve the wines. Here are the classic guidelines:

- White wine before red wine
- Light wine before heavy wine
- Dry wine before sweet wine
- Simple wine before complex, richly flavored wine

Each of these principles operates independently. You needn't go crazy trying to follow all of them together, or you'll be able to drink nothing but light, dry, simple whites and heavy, complex, sweet reds!

First things first

Even if you don't plan to serve hors d'oeuvres, you'll probably want to offer your guests a drink when they arrive to set a relaxing tone for the evening. We like to serve Champagne (notice the capital C) as the apéritif because opening the bottle is a ceremony that brings together everyone in the group. Champagne honors your guests. And a glass of Champagne is compelling enough that to spend a thoughtful moment tasting it doesn't seem rude; even people who think it's absurd to talk about wine understand that Champagne is too special to be ignored.

How much is enough

The necessary quantity of each wine depends on all sorts of issues, including the number of wines you serve (if you serve several, you need less of each), the pace of service (if you plan a long, leisurely meal, you'll need more of each wine), and the size of your wine glasses. If you're using oversized glasses, you need more of each wine, because it's easy to pour more than you realize into each glass.

Assuming a full-blown dinner that includes an apéritif wine, two wines with dinner, and another with cheese — and guests who all drink moderately — we recommend that you plan to have one bottle of each wine for every four people. That gives each person four ounces of each wine, with plenty left over in the 25-ounce bottle for refills. When serving two wines, plan one bottle of each wine per couple.

One simpler rule is to figure, in total, a full bottle of wine per guest (total consumption). That quantity may sound high, but if your dinner is spread over several hours and you're serving a lot of food, the quantity really isn't immoderate. If you're concerned that your guests might overindulge, be sure that their water glasses are always full so that they have an alternative to automatically reaching for the wine.

If your dinner party is special enough to have several food courses and several wines, we recommend giving each guest a separate glass for each wine. The glasses can be different for each wine, or they can be alike. All those glasses really look festive on the table. And with a separate glass for each wine, no guest feels compelled to empty each glass before going on to the next wine. (You also can tell at a glance who is drinking the wine and who isn't really interested in it, and you can adjust your pouring accordingly.)

Chapter 7

Marrying Wine with Food

In This Chapter

- Predictable reactions between wines and foods
- Guiding principles for matchmakers
- Classic combos that still work

Every now and then, we encounter a wine that stops us dead in our tracks. That wine is so sensational that we lose all interest in anything but that wine. We drink the wine with intent appreciation, trying to memorize the taste. We wouldn't dream of diluting its perfection with a mouthful of food.

But 999 times out of 1,000, we drink our wine with food. Wine is meant to go with food. And good food is meant to go with wine.

Matchmaker, Matchmaker . . .

Good. We've settled that. Wine goes with food, and food goes with wine. Any questions?

Of course we're being facetious. Thousands of wines exist in the world, and every wine is different. Thousands of basic foods exist in the world as well, each different — not to mention the infinite combinations of foods in prepared dishes (what we really eat). In reality, food-with-wine is about as simple an issue as boy-meets-girl.

The dynamics of food and wine

Every dish is dynamic — it's made up of several ingredients and flavors that interact to create a (more or less) delicious whole. Every wine is dynamic in exactly the same way. When food and wine combine in your mouth, the dynamics of each change; the result is completely individual to each dish-and-wine combination. (Dare we also mention that we each use our individual palates to judge the success of each combination? No wonder we have no rules!)

When wine meets food, several things can happen:

- The food can exaggerate a characteristic of the wine. For example, if you eat walnuts (which are tannic) with a tannic red wine, such as a Bordeaux, the wine tastes so dry and astringent that most people would consider it undrinkable.
- The food can diminish a characteristic of the wine. Protein diminishes tannin, for example, and an overly-tannic red wine — unpleasant on its own — could be delightful with rare steak or roast beef.
- The flavor intensity of the food can obliterate the wine's flavor or vice versa. If you've ever drunk a big, rich red wine with a delicate filet of sole, you've had this experience firsthand.
- The wine can contribute new flavors to the dish. For example, a red Zinfandel that's gushing with berry fruit can bring its berry flavors to the dish, as if another ingredient had been added.
- The combination of wine and food can create an unwelcome third-party flavor that wasn't in either the wine or the food originally; we get a metallic flavor when we eat plain white-meat turkey with red Bordeaux.
- The food and wine can interact perfectly, creating a sensational taste experience that is greater than the food or the wine alone. (This scenario is what we hope will happen every time we eat and drink, but it's as rare as a show-stopping dish.)

Fortunately, what happens between food and wine is not haphazard. Certain elements of food react in predictable ways with certain elements of wine, giving us a fighting chance at making successful matches. The major components of wine (alcohol, sweetness, acid, and tannin) relate to the basic tastes of food (sweetness, sourness, bitterness, and saltiness) the same way that the principle of balance in wine operates: Some of the elements exaggerate each other, and some of them compensate for each other. (Refer to the discussion of balance in Chapter 2.)

Here are some ways that food and wine interact, based on the components of the wine. Each wine and each dish has more than one component, and the simple relationships we describe can be complicated by other elements in the wine or the food. Whether a wine is considered tannic, sweet, acidic, or high in alcohol depends on its dominant component. (Refer to Chapter 2.)

Tannic wines

Tannic wines include most wines based on the Cabernet Sauvignon grape (including red Bordeaux), northern Rhône reds, Barolo and Barbaresco, and any wine — white or red — that has become tannic from aging in new oak barrels. These wines

- Can diminish the perception of sweetness in a food.
- Can taste softer and less tannic when served with protein-rich, fatty foods, such as steak or cheese.
- Can taste less bitter when paired with salty foods.
- Can taste astringent, or mouth-drying, when drunk with spicy-hot foods.

The fifth wheel

Common wisdom was that humans can perceive four basic tastes: sweet, sour, salty, and bitter. But people who study food have concluded that a fifth taste exists. This taste is called *umami* (pronounced *oo MAH me*), and it is associated with a savory character in foods. Shellfish, oily fish, meats, and cheeses are some foods high in umami taste.

Umami-rich foods can increase the sensation of bitterness in wines served with them. To counteract this effect, try adding something salty (such as salt itself) or sour (such as vinegar) to your dish. Although this suggestion defies the adage that vinegar and wine don't get along, the results are the proof of the pudding.

Sweet wines

Some wines that often have some sweetness include most inexpensive California white wines, White Zinfandel, many Rieslings (unless they're labeled "dry" or "trocken"), and medium-dry Vouvray. Sweet wines also include dessert wines such as Port, sweetened Sherries, and late-harvest wines. These wines

- Can taste less sweet, but fruitier, when matched with salty foods.
- Can make salty foods more appealing.
- Can go well with sweet foods.

Acidic wines

Acidic wines include most Italian white wines; Sancerre, Pouilly-Fumé, and Chablis; traditionally-made red wines from Rioja; most dry Rieslings; and wines based on Sauvignon Blanc that are fully dry. These wines

- Can taste less acidic when served with salty foods.
- Can taste less acidic when served with slightly sweet foods.
- Can make foods taste slightly saltier.
- Can counterbalance oily or fatty heaviness in food.

High-alcohol wines

High alcohol wines include many California wines, both white and red; southern Rhône whites and reds; Barolo and Barbaresco; fortified wines such as Port and Sherry; and most wines produced from grapes grown in warm climates. These wines

- Can overwhelm lightly flavored or delicate dishes.
- Can go well with slightly sweet foods.

Birds of a feather, or opposites attract?

Two principles can help in matching wine with food: the complementary principle and the contrast principle. The complementary principle involves choosing a wine that is similar in some way to the dish you're planning to serve, while the contrast principle (not surprisingly) involves combining foods with wines that are dissimilar to them in some way.

The characteristics of a wine that can either resemble or contrast with the characteristics of a dish are

- **The wine's flavors.** Earthy, herbal, fruity, vegetal, and so on
- **The intensity of flavor in the wine.** Weak flavor intensity, moderately flavorful, or very flavorful
- **The wine's texture.** Crisp and firm, or soft and supple
- **The weight of the wine.** Light-bodied, medium-bodied, or full-bodied

You probably use the complementary principle often without realizing it: You choose a light-bodied wine to go with a light dish, a medium-bodied wine to go with a fuller dish, and a full-bodied wine to go with a heavy dish. Some other examples of the complementary principle in action are

- **Dishes with flavors that resemble those in the wine.** Think about the flavors in a dish the same way you think about the flavors in wine — as families of flavors. If a dish has mushrooms, it has an earthy flavor; if a dish has citrus or other elements of fruit, it has a fruity flavor (and so on). Then consider which wines would offer their own earthy flavor, fruity flavor, herbal flavor, spicy flavor, or whatever. The earthy flavors of white Burgundy complement risotto with mushrooms, for example, and an herbal Sancerre complements chicken breast with fresh herbs.
- **Foods with texture similar to that of the wine.** A California Chardonnay with a creamy, rich texture could match the rich, soft texture of lobster, for example.
- **Foods and wines whose intensity of flavor match.** A very flavorful Asian stir-fry or Tex-Mex dish would be at home with a very flavorful (rather than a subtle) wine.

The contrast principle seeks to find flavors or texture in a wine that are not in a dish, but that would enhance the dish. A dish of fish or chicken in a rich cream and butter sauce, for example, might be matched with a dry Vouvray, a white wine whose crispness (thanks to its uplifting, high acidity) would counterbalance the heaviness of the dish. A dish with earthy flavors such as portobello mushrooms and fresh fava beans (or potatoes and black truffles) might contrast nicely with the pure fruit flavor of an Alsace Riesling.

In order to apply either principle, of course, you have to have a good idea of what the food is going to taste like and what various wines taste like. That second part can be a real stumbling block for people who don't devote every ounce of their free energy to learning about wine. The solution is to ask your wine merchant. A retailer might not have the world's greatest knack in wine and food pairings (then again, he or she might), but at least he should know what his wines taste like.

The wisdom of the ages

In wine-and-food terms, it pays to know the classic pairings because they work, and they're a sure thing. Here are some famous and reliable combinations:

- Oysters and Chablis
- Port with walnuts and Stilton cheese
- Salmon with Pinot Noir
- Amarone with Gorgonzola cheese
- Grilled fish with Vinho Verde
- Foie gras with Sauternes or with late-harvest Gewürztraminer
- Braised beef with Barolo
- Grilled chicken with Beaujolais
- Toasted almonds or green olives with fino or manzanilla Sherry
- Goat cheese with Sancerre or Pouilly-Fumé
- Dark chocolate with California Cabernet Sauvignon

Index

• A •

• B •

• C •

• D •

• E •

• F •

• G •

• H •

• I •

• L •

• M •

• N •

• P •

• Q •

• R •

• S •

• T •

• U •

• V •

• W •

• Y •

• Z •